HISTORY

AND

PROGRESS OF EDUCATION,

FROM

THE EARLIEST TIMES TO THE PRESENT.

INTENDED AS

A MANUAL FOR TEACHERS AND STUDENTS.

BY PHILOBIBLIUS. (Linus P. Brockett

WITH AN INTRODUCTION BY

HENRY BARNARD, LL. D.,

CHANCELLOR OF THE UNIVERSITY OF WISCONSIN.

A. S. BARNES & COMPANY,

NEW YORK AND CHICAGO.

PREFACE.

In offering to the public the accompanying "History of Education," the writer begs leave to say, that it has been his object rather to prepare a manual for the student, than a work of greater pretension for the mere literary man. The field is almost wholly untrodden in our own language, the very brief and imperfect little treatise of Schmidt being, it is believed, the only work professedly devoted to this topic, which is accessible to those who read English only. The works of Fritz, De Riancy, De Viriville, Schwarz, and Niemeyer, in French and German, are valuable; but of these, only that of De Viriville, which is confined to European, and particularly to French education, is at all recent; and all of them view the subject too exclusively from the continental stand-point. Hallam's *History of Literature* is invaluable for the period of which it treats, and throws more light on the educational condition of Great Britain, up to the eighteenth century, than any other work. The complete history of education in the United States is yet to be written; let us hope that the life and health of the eminent scholar * who has so long been engaged in its preparation, may be spared, till he shall have completed a work which cannot fail greatly to enhance his already exalted reputation. Meantime, we have been able to glean from the pages of the *American Journal of Education*, and other educational periodicals, sufficient facts to answer the purpose of our manual.

---

* Hon. Henry Barnard.

The preparation of this manual has been a work of severe and protracted toil; it would have been far easier to have made it much larger; and it might have suited a few of our readers better, had we given references to the authorities quoted, at the foot of each page; but, mindful of our purpose, we have studied condensation, and, while verifying with the utmost care every reference, have deemed a bibliographical list of authorities, at the close of the work, sufficient, and more unpretending than a pompous array of foot-notes, which should refer to works, many of which not one reader in a thousand could consult.

The writer cannot, in justice to his own feelings, close this preface without acknowledging his obligations to Hon. Henry Barnard for many kindnesses received in the preparation of this volume; and especially for free access to his valuable library, the most extensive, in this specialty, in the United States. Much of what is valuable in the work, is due to this kindly assistance; for any faults of style, or errors of fact, which may be found in it, the writer is alone responsible.

CONTENTS.

CHAPTER IX.

CHAPTER X.

CHAPTER XI.

CHAPTER XII.

CHAPTER XIII.

CHAPTER XIV.

CHAPTER XV.

CHAPTER XVI.

CHAPTER XVII.

CHAPTER XXII.

CHAPTER XXIII.

CHAPTER XXIV.

INTRODUCTION.

In an age so peculiarly and eagerly progressive as the present, the profound saying of Solomon, that "There is no new thing under the sun," is eminently liable to be forgotten; and investigators and experimenters, absorbed in what they are doing, and still more in what they desire and hope to do, utterly forget that any thing has ever been done before.

Yet no subject, now interesting or important, can be adequately understood, or further investigated, unless proper pains be first bestowed upon its history. The truth of this proposition is so clear, in relation to mechanic arts and the various departments of natural science, that it scarcely needs illustration. The machinist, for example, is compelled, by the very course of the labors of his apprenticeship, to master those results of all the centuries of thought, of imagination, and of tireless exertion, which are so wonderfully exemplified in every great workshop. He cannot, in the nature of things, re-invent and construct for sale the imperfect steam-engine of Newcomen, or the comparatively clumsy early power-looms of Arkwright. The watchmaker could not sell clepsydras, nor "Nuremberg eggs;" he absolutely *must* avail himself of the results of that long train of ingenious and skillful men, whose latest representatives are our own Yankee clock and watch manufacturers. In these cases there is neither doubt nor danger. The tendency of trade, the weight of gain, an influence as universal and unerring as gravitation, determines the mechanic. In the market, it is only the latest improvement which commands a sale; and the steady force of the law of supply and demand, and the sleepless instinct of gain, is a sufficient warrant that, while superfluities are dropped, and improvements are adopted, no re-invention of an exploded contrivance, nor retrogression to an older and more imperfect condition, will be allowed.

The same is true in the opposite pursuit of the most abstract philosophy. It is impossible to conceive of any person's attempting to put forth a system of philosophical belief, who shall not first have made, not perhaps the best use, but at all events his own use, of the whole long series of philosophers, from Aristotle to Sir William Hamilton. For the grade of intellect and cultivation which admits him to conceive of such a system, renders any other supposition impossible. And no preface is more unfailing, or more determinate in substance, than the historical view in which the modern philosopher upsets the theories of all his predecessors, creating, like an Asiatic conqueror, a wide-spread desert in which to erect his throne.

There is no department of human exertion, however, in which this preliminary historical knowledge is so necessary as in education. For this there is both a general and a special reason. The education of a people bears a constant and most pre-eminently influential relation to its attainments and excellences—physical, mental, and moral. The national education is at once a cause and an effect of the national character; and, accordingly, the history of education affords the only ready and perfect key to the history of the human race, and of each nation in it,—an unfailing standard for estimating its advance or retreat upon the line of human progress.

But the special reason just alluded to, is yet more in point at this time. It is, that there is no department of human exertion whose annals are more brilliant with displays of industry, talent, and genius, whether successful or unsuccessful; and consequently none in which a reference to the past will afford such abundant materials for improvement in the present.

In our own country all this pre-eminent truth, regarding education, is again still more pre-eminently true. Nowhere among civilized nations is the business of education pursued with such utter lack of system, such complete, unsympathizing, independent, self-dependent isolation of effort,—though yet with a fervor, devotion, energy, and natural capacity almost equally unrivaled.

Yet our system of education has, nevertheless, been so universally and efficiently successful as a *practical* system—or, to state more correctly what is a cotemporary rather than a resulting fact, the men and communities trained under it have been, and are, characterized by so many excellences—as to furnish what seems a conclusive refutation of the positions taken.

But the reason of this is not to be looked for in the system itself. It can only be found by means of a broad estimate of the total influence of all the social, political, and religious circumstances of our people. Our men and women grow up within a home atmosphere of purity, of active thought and intelligent cultivation; all their powers are keenly stimulated by national prosperity, unlimited freedom in all good endeavors, and a social equality absolutely ideal in its perfection; and they are, nevertheless, living under the wholesome though almost unfelt restraints of laws and governments adapted to a free and good people, with a wisdom only less than divine. And men and women growing up under such circumstances, will commonly become good and useful and intelligent members of the commonwealth, by virtue of forces which might even be termed independent of a few years' schooling, were it not that we know how greatly the school training aids, fortifies, confirms, and enhances all the good results of the other influences of life.

The comparatively high standard of mental and moral attainment reached by the graduates of our educational institutions, is not a proof that our educators do not need the same aids, and the same use of them, as those of other countries. Because they succeed astonishingly well without them, it would be folly to argue that they would not succeed still far better with them; and if this is so, it is unnecessary to prove at length that it is a duty to use them.

The educators of the United States—to resume the course of remark interrupted by this reference to the apparent actual results of their labors—are even peculiarly destitute of the advantages derivable from a competent knowledge of the history of education. Deprived, as most of them are and must be, of any thing like a scientific training in their profession, and thus left to make the best use in their power of their own recollections of school-days, of brief and superficial observation, and of short courses of technical instruction at teachers' institutes or normal schools, they are liable to all the errors of inexperience and youth. And by just as much as they are ardently interested, by just as much as their minds are full of their occupation, and fruitful in suggestions of principles and methods for prosecuting it, by precisely so much are they more liable to re-invent modes and ideas which have been tried and given up before, and thus to spend precious months, or years even, in pursuing and detecting errors which a small knowledge of the history of their profession would have prevented them from practicing for a moment, and would have taught them carefully to avoid.

A self-taught modern geometer, who, in the forests of the West, should re-discover the solution of the Pythagorean problem,—or a mathematician who should, in solitary, ignorant study, re-invent the common system of logarithms or the calculus, might possess a genius as great, possibly, as Pythagoras, or Napier, or Newton. But the vain pomposity of a self-taught genius is proverbial. The manner of his announcement of his discovery, if not the matter of it, would insure him infinite ridicule; and his wisest friends could furnish him no consolation better than their regrets that, instead of painfully laboring through those difficult ways, he had not exercised the privilege and the duty of the judicious student, passed forward to the existing limits of knowledge by the friendly aid of his predecessors, and then expended his powers, at once for his own real fame and for the actual good of his race, by bravely plunging forward into the infinite realms of the unknown, and adding a new province to the empires of human thought.

Instances of the wasteful method of re-discovery here alluded to, often come under the notice of those whose reading has made them acquainted with educational history. It is unnecessary to cite in this place more than one or two of these, for illustration's sake. Within a few years, the use of newspapers in schools, in the place of reading-books, has been recommended in various quarters, as a modern invention. It is modern only in the same sense in which newspapers are modern; for that great educator and excellent man, John Amos Comenius, recommended the same use of a gazette published in Holland, or of some periodical of similar character, about the year 1640, when newspapers were first struggling into existence. The various uses of apparatus, of school museums and collections of natural history, of the whole circle of actual objects which are, at the present day, more and more urged, and brought into use to illustrate and enforce the oral instructions of the teacher, were all elaborately advocated, in principle, and to a great extent in detail, by the same Comenius, and again, with vastly greater good fortune and success, after the lapse of a century and a half, by Pestalozzi. Indeed, it is little or no exaggeration to say that the whole range of the "modern improvements" in instruction, which are now in progress among us, which are doing so useful a work, and which are regarded by their advocates and exemplifiers with so much just complacency, will be found to have been conceived, and often discussed and elaborated at great length, seventy years ago, by the little company of ardent and laborious teachers who, with Pestalozzi, did so great a work at Burgdorf and Yverdun.

But this presentation of the point under discussion will suffice; and its length would even be superfluous, were it not for the singular exception to the good old rule of judging from experience, which has prevailed in the case of education.

It is the design of the present work to furnish such an account of the various systems of education which have characterized races, or have enjoyed a successive pre-eminence during the historical ages of the world, as shall afford the student a competent general view of their spirit and practice. Its limits, of course, preclude that fullness of detail, and length of discussion, which would be necessary to an exhaustive treatment of the subject, or to any endeavor after such treatment. That task would require a work many times more voluminous than the present; for the great problems of education are either identical, or inextricably and influentially interwoven, with all the great problems of human life and action. The views which are here given are intended to possess such a measure of completeness as may insure their competent accuracy, and as will enable the reader to form a fair and intelligent judgment upon the leading practical questions of education. It traces their history in practice, from nation to nation, and from age to age; and, even if some more zealous student should fail to find the work as encyclopedic as he might desire, it will afford him much food for thought, and may prove a most valuable stimulus to further investigation. As the pioneer American work in its department, it may legitimately both bespeak kind consideration and demand credit. And if it shall, at some future time, point out the way for a more voluminous historian to erect a more stately and extensive structure of narrative and exposition, this alone will be no small advantage and no small praise.

HENRY BARNARD.

Madison, Wis., *Oct.*, 1859.

HISTORY

AND

PROGRESS OF EDUCATION.

CHAPTER I.

Definition.—Intellectual and physical training in the antediluvian period.—The ages after the Flood.—Circumstances favoring civilization, and intellectual development.—Education in India.—Caste.—Education denied to the lower castes, and to women.

THE origin of the word *education* (*educo*, I lead or draw out), implies the idea of development, and hence we include in the term education, whatever tends to develop the physical, the intellectual, or the moral powers of man. In this extended sense, it commences with the birth of the infant, continues through life, and, we have reason to believe, progresses through the future state of being. It embraces the training of the physical powers, the instruction and improvement of the intellectual faculties, and the culture of the moral affections and emotions. We are accustomed, therefore, to speak of physical, intellectual, and moral or religious education.

In a more restricted sense, however, education is sometimes used to signify only the training of the intellect, or sometimes of the intellect and moral nature combined. In attempting to give a brief historical sketch of the progress of education, we shall use the term mainly in the latter sense; for among the earlier nations, the priests were, for the most part, the only teachers, and instruction and worship were so intimately associated, that it would be impossible to sever them, while the cultivation of the physical powers was left to nature, and to the circumstances and necessities of each race.

In the early history of mankind, the instincts were, of course, first developed; the body must be protected from atmospheric changes, and the natural clothing of beasts afforded the means of accomplishing this; shelter from the sun and rain, and protection from wild beasts were the next necessity, and for this purpose, booths made from the branches of trees, or huts from their trunks (both of which seem to have preceded tents, which, however, were soon invented, for the convenience of the shepherd and herdsman), were constructed; the domestication of some of the animal tribes, and their protection from beasts of prey, came next in order; and for this purpose, weapons, which, even prior to the Deluge, seem to have been made of iron or copper, were required; and thus the mere physical necessities of man were satisfied

But even at this early period, in the seventh generation from Adam, the intellectual tastes began to be cultivated: for we find that the love of music led, in the case of Jubal, to the invention of some rude instruments of music, probably, as the Hebrew words imply, the lyre and the Pandean pipe. Of the further progress of the antediluvians in the arts and sciences, the sacred record gives us little information; we learn, indeed, that they had some rude notions of architecture, and some knowledge of the use of tools, for the construction of a vessel, so gigantic in size as the ark, would require these. The language of the original would also imply that some means had been devised for transmitting light to the interior of this vast structure, the word translated windows, implying the ideas of brilliancy and transparency; this may have been, and probably was, some membranous substance, or possibly mica, but its use indicated a very considerable advance from the savage state. Nor can we suppose that the antediluvians, and especially the descendants of Seth, lacked religious culture.

The distinction made in regard to the sacrifices of Cain and Abel, in itself implies a somewhat extended course of religious instruction. The offering of the lamb indicated evidently the knowledge of its typical character, and involved the idea of expiatory sacrifice. The high religious character of Enoch could not have been attained by special revelation solely; and the recollections of the lost Paradise, and of intercourse with angelic beings, might well have been communicated to him by Adam, who was his cotemporary during the greater part of his life. Nor do the gigantic crimes which led to the destruction of the antediluvian world, imply necessarily a want of intellectual culture, for analogy shows that, in all ages of the world, high intellectual attainment, when unrestrained by moral motives, has been productive of the grossest crimes.

Passing by, however, any further consideration of the mental condition of the races prior to the flood, we come to post-diluvian times, concerning which we have more definite information. The descendants of Noah, settling, at first, on the fertile plains lying between the Euphrates and Tigris, in the course of a few centuries sent forth colonies, to India, to China and perhaps Japan, and to Egypt and Ethiopia. Some of these colonies, in process of time, outstripped the parent stock in intellectual progress. Recent discoveries, however, demonstrate that, at a very early period, the Assyrians and Babylonians—who, if not themselves the parent stock, were in constant communication with the descendants of those who remained on the plains of Shinar—had a written language, and understood many of the arts and sciences.

Certain conditions seem to have been necessary to any considerable intellectual progress among the early nations of the world, and by a knowledge of the existence or non-existence of these, it is comparatively easy to determine whether any nation had, or had not, emerged from barbarism. Where the soil was highly fertile, and food abundant, and either from conquest, or as a result of famine, as in Egypt, the lands were owned by the king and his immediate associates or nobles, thus forming a higher class in society, possessing the power of governing and controlling the great mass of the population, the governing class would usually advance in civilization and intellectual culture. This would certainly be the case, if, from their location, they were not addicted to war, and if, moreover, they had established a system of religion, which conferred special privileges on the nobles and priests.

Historians have usually considered the inhabitants of India as by far the most highly educated of all the early nations, and probably justly, since in their case all these circumstances coincided to give them the opportunity for mental development. The fertility of their soil was such as to encourage the most rapid increase of population. From the earliest period the lands were considered the property of the higher classes; desolating wars were, in their early history, of rare occurrence, and their religious system, which, in itself, exhibited the marks of extraordinary genius, divided the people into castes, of which the lowest or laboring caste (the Sudras), comprising the great mass of the people, were consigned to the lowest degradation, and the most abject servitude to those above them. Still, degraded as these were, there was a class below them, the Pariahs or outcasts, who were cut off from the sympathies of their kind, and to look upon whom entailed ceremonial defilement.

The three upper castes, comprising the Brahmins, or priestly order, the warriors, and the commercial or mercantile class, were allowed privileges of education, to which it was sacrilege for the Sudras, or laboring class, to aspire—but, even in their case, the education was esoteric and exoteric; and while all were admitted to exoteric privileges, including the study of language, and some rudiments of science, poetry, the popular religious doctrines, philosophy, history, astronomy, jurisprudence, and some slight medical knowledge, the Brahmins alone were admitted to the esoteric studies, which included the higher mythology, and in some cases the mysteries of their most sacred shrines, mathematics, and astrology.

It is not to be supposed, however, that these studies were all taught in the earliest periods of their history, or that they approached in extent or accuracy to the sciences we call by the same names. Their cosmogony was absurd and childish, their history mostly fabulous, their astronomy confined to some slight knowledge of the movements of the heavenly bodies. But even this education, meager as it was, was withheld, most carefully, from the great mass of the people: if the Sudra, longing for instruction, dared to listen to the reading of the sacred books, in which all the science of the time was concentrated, burning oil was to be poured into his ears; if he attempted to commit the words to memory, he was to be put to death, and the Brahmin who should attempt to teach him was threatened with perdition. These Sudras are estimated by Ward as comprising three-fourths of the Hindoo people.

Strict as these laws were in prohibiting the instruction of the lowest caste, they were not less strict in defining the position of woman—a position, if possible, more degrading than that of the Sudra. It was a terrible disgrace for a woman to have learned to read, and the avowal of that knowledge was sufficient to class her with the most abandoned of her sex.

Her duties and attainments were only such as would conduce to the mere physical comfort of her lord and master; and when he died, cruelly as he might have treated her, custom required that she should sacrifice her life for him, on the funeral pile, especially if he were a Brahmin.

CHAPTER II.

Education in Egypt and Ethiopia.—Caste.—Instruction exoteric and esoteric.—Females of the higher castes educated.—Education confined to the higher castes.—The masses degraded and oppressed.—Egypt the seat of the highest learning at a later period.—Education among the Chinese.—Schools.—System of instruction.—Education a necessary qualification for high official station.—Literary honors and degrees.—Much of this education only intended to develop the memory.—Chinese keys, for examinations.

Let us turn next to Egypt and Ethiopia, or, as it is called in modern times, Abyssinia. We find here the system of education and of religion bearing so strong a resemblance (the result probably of their common origin, and similar circumstances) to that of India, that many writers have supposed Egypt to have been settled by an Indian colony. Aside, however, from the improbability of a colony having come from a region so remote, there were differences in their religious and educational systems, sufficiently marked to preclude such a theory.

The division of caste existed among the

Egyptians, and there were three of the privileged classes—priests, warriors, and professional men, including judges, architects, writers, and perhaps also physicians. The priests held the real power of the nation in their hands, though the monarch was generally chosen from the warrior class. Upon these three classes was bestowed most of the education of the country, an education which, like that of India, was exoteric and esoteric; the former including a knowledge of the demotic or common mode of writing (while the hieroglyphic, or sacred, was confined to the priestly class alone), geometry, and mensuration of land—both sciences rendered necessary by the frequent changes induced by the overflowing of the Nile; arithmetic, astronomy, chemistry, in which they were more proficient than any other of the nations of antiquity; architecture, sculpture, painting, music, and, where they designed practicing it, a system of medicine. The *abacus*, a kind of numeral frame, in which stones were used for arithmetical processes, was in common use.

The children of the priests were also instructed in the sacred mysteries and in the higher mathematics, and made familiar with the hieroglyphic language, and the sciences and mysteries concealed in its literature. The female children of the higher classes, and particularly of the priests, were allowed to acquire an education, and many of them availed themselves of the opportunity. The children of the royal family were carefully instructed, and were only allowed to have as companions the most intelligent of the youth of the priestly class.

The priests, as the instructors of the nation, were required to lead an abstemious and virtuous life, were allowed to have but one wife, and were forbidden all those articles of food which would make them gross or indolent. The same regimen was observed with their pupils. The plainest fare, and the hardest of beds, were the portion of the youth who were acquiring an education. The lands of the country were all held by the privileged castes.

The lower orders, comprising the artificers,

the agriculturists, and the herdsmen, except the swineherds (who constituted a *Pariah* class, and were forbidden education, or the privilege of visiting the temples), were allowed but little education, and that little was usually communicated by their parents, or near relatives. They were not cut off, like the Sudras in India, from all instruction, but were generally taught (both males and females) reading the demotic character and arithmetic, as necessary for the purposes of trade, in which the women engaged oftener than the men; they were also instructed in the art, trade, or business which their parents had followed, and which they were expected to practice. If agriculturists, they were obliged to pay one-fourth of the produce of their land to the proprietors of the soil, who were usually either members of the reigning family or of the priestly caste. During the reign of the Shepherd Kings and the Pyramid builders, the mass of the people were in the most abject condition, many hundreds of thousands of them being compelled to undergo the severest hardships, in the erection of the pyramids; but subsequently their condition was much ameliorated.

At a later period in the history of Egypt, when the Greek civilization, which originated in Egypt, but had greatly improved and advanced under the wise measures of the Greek philosophers and law-givers, was reintroduced there, by Alexander the Great and his successors, Alexandria and the other cities of the Delta became as renowned for their schools of philosophy and science, as Thebes, Memphis, and Heliopolis had been, in earlier times, for the schools of the priests. The dynasty of the Ptolemies was renowned for its devotion to science and literature, and the vast libraries of the Bruchion and the Serapeum at Alexandria, were the most remarkable monuments of the learning of the period.

The Chinese and Japanese deserve a passing notice for their early systems of education. The exact period at which these nations emerged from barbarism can not be ascertained, for the traditions of a remote antiquity are always mingled with fable; but that it could hardly have been much later than the intellectual development of the Hindoo and Egyptian nations seems evident. The most renowned sage of the Chinese, Con-fut-see, who flourished about 550 B. C., expressly disclaims having originated any of the views he promulgated; he had only, he said, attempted to revive the doctrines of the ancient sages of the nation, which in the long lapse of ages had fallen into desuetude. The regulations in regard to education, which he thus resuscitated, and which were practiced in their spirit for many years, as they now are in form, were in many respects admirable, and greatly in advance of those of the other nations at that early period.

The course of instruction, intended for boys of all classes, was commenced in the family at an early age; they were taught to reverence their parents and ancestors, to repeat certain precepts of morality, and to commit some extracts from the Chi-King and other ancient books to memory; they were also taught to count, up to 10,000, and instructed in the elements of grammar. At the age of five or six years, they were sent to school. Here they were required to make, on entering, their obeisance, first to the holy Con-fut-see, or before his time to some earlier sage, and next, to their teacher. This done, the lessons of the day were to be studied. These consisted to a great extent of memoritic exercises, chirography, chanting odes from the Chi-King or other text-books, narration and explanation of historical events, and some further instruction in arithmetic. Moral instruction was carefully mingled with intellectual, and a strict, though not cruel, discipline maintained.

On returning home, they were required to salute, first, the domestic spirits, then their ancestors, and afterward their parents and relatives, and any strangers who might be present. The course of instruction, where the attendance was constant, and the child studious, might be completed in three years, but it was usually prolonged beyond this. These schools seem not to have been supported by the general government, but by the local authorities. Female children were not admitted to them, but they were very generally taught to read, write, and sing. A higher course of instruction was provided by the government for the children of the nobles and wealthier classes, as well as for those of marked promise in the ordinary schools.

In no nation of ancient or modern times, with possibly the exception of Prussia, has education been the means of official promotion as much as among the Chinese. In each considerable city, there was a seminary of high grade, intended for the instruction of young men who wished to qualify themselves for official stations. The candidates for admission into these schools, were obliged to pass an examination conducted by the governor of the city, and after attendance upon the seminary they were again examined by the governor of a city of the first magnitude; when, if able to pass, they were permitted to enter the imperial college at Pekin, and remained for three years, when they could, by passing a further examination, receive an appointment to some inferior office. But a very small proportion of those who offered themselves were able to pass the very strict examination.

A mandarin of high rank was every year deputed to hold examinations, in the larger cities, of those who aspired to the first degree in the arts, called by the Chinese Liroutsay. From each company of four hundred candidates, fifteen were selected who passed the best examination, after ten trials, on whom the degree was conferred. This degree was accompanied with some civil privileges, one of the most considerable of which was, exemption from chastisement with the bamboo. Those who had attained to this degree, were allowed to compete at the triennial examination, at Pekin, for the higher degree, and if they succeeded in passing the severe and repeated examinations, received it, and the following year passed, if they chose, a third examination, at the capital, on which, if successful, they received the degree of Tsin-tse, which answers to our Doctor of Laws. The recipient of this title was eligible to the most important offices, and could enjoy, at the pleasure of the Emperor, the title of Han-Lin, the highest of all literary titles.

The investigations of recent travelers and missionaries, however, prove, that a very large portion of the studies on which the Chinese lay so much stress, consisted of mere repetitions of long lists of names, or of works, whose meaning was seldom comprehended by the student. The mathematical sciences, beyond the simple rules of arithmetic, received but little attention, and no language except Chinese was studied, nor had they made much progress in the physical sciences. Keys, or answers to the questions usually propounded, prepared on small slips of paper, were also frequently procured by the candidates. A specimen of these is now in the library of Yale College.

CHAPTER III.

The Japanese.—Their scientific discoveries.—Education of prostitutes. —Ancient Babylonians and Assyrians.—Evidence of their educational condition afforded by recent discoveries.—Ancient Persians. —Parsees or Fire Worshipers.—Magi.—Their position.—Xenophon's account of education in the time of Cyrus.—The four classes. —This education confined to those possessing some property.—Female degradation.—Little accomplished for education by Zartusht or Zoroaster.

THE Japanese seem to have had a system of education superior to the Chinese, pursuing a wider and more liberal course of scientific studies, and acquiring the languages of some other nations. Their academies of science, as well as their professional schools, were quite respectable. From Commodore Perry's narrative, it appears that they understand the preparation of a kind of stereotype plates, from which their books are printed; that they adopted, centuries ago, a decimal system of weights and measures, and that in many of the arts and sciences, requiring no inconsiderable chemical skill, they are proficient.

Females receive some education, and those who are destined to an abandoned life, of whom there are vast numbers, are usually well taught in the literature and poetry of the country, that they may thus be rendered more attractive.

Of the early inhabitants of the plain of Shinar and the land lying between the Euphrates and Tigris, the Mesopotamia of the Scriptures, and the vast empires of Babylon and Assyria, our information is scanty, derived mainly from the Scripture record and the recent explorations of Layard, Rawlinson, Taylor, Loftus, and others. That they had attained, at a period seven or eight centuries after the flood, to a high degree of civilization, is evident from the remains which explorers have found there. Their monuments, their rooms, stairways, and tablets, all covered with inscriptions, in the cuneiform character, mostly historical; their bank or treasury notes, found by Mr. Loftus, in the form of clay tablets; their complex mode of numeration, reckoning by tens and by sixties; their skill in sculpture, in architecture, and in horticulture; the existence of a class of wise men or *magi*, selected for their profound attainments in chemistry, astronomy, astrology, and other mystic arts, all indicate a nation which had made very considerable advances in education.

Yet we find, on the other hand, a religion of the most debasing and brutal character, pandering to the indulgence of every lust, and inciting to the most bloody and cruel sacrifices; child-murder very generally practiced, human sacrifices offered to idols, and even parents casting their own children into the red-hot arms of the brazen statue of the Fire-God. From these and other circumstances, we can but derive the conclusion that education was confined to the few, and those of the highest rank, while the masses were unenlightened.

The data for determining the educational condition of the ancient Persians, are much more full and satisfactory. The Zend-Avesta, or sacred book of the Parsees, or Fire Worshipers, the descendants of the ancient Per sians, which is ascribed, though with somewhat doubtful probability, to *Zartusht*, the Zoroaster of the Greeks, contains the material for forming a tolerably accurate idea of the early education of that nation. The descendants of Elam, the son of Shem, who were the earliest inhabitants of Persia, seem to have been a simple pastoral people, who had retained, in greater purity than most of the adjacent nations, the religious principles handed down to them by their ancestor, but possessing little intellectual culture.

In the lapse of ages, at a period cotemporary with that of the patriarch Job, the Tzabeans, acknowledged idolaters and polytheists, attained the ascendency over the simple descendants of Elam, who had hitherto reared no idols, but regarded with reverence the sun, as the emblem of Divinity, the air, the earth, and the water as the means by which the power of the Divinity was displayed; in their train followed the MAGI, a body of wise men who probably originated in Chaldea, and who for ages ruled the Persians, by the force of their intellect alone. They abolished the worship of idols, but retained the use of fire as the only symbol of deity. With intellects quickened by their active exercise, they became the inventors, the discoverers, the men of science of the nation, in which they were nevertheless foreigners and strangers. Debarred, by the jealousy of the people, from the throne or from high office, as well as from the marts of trade, they yet managed to be for ages the governing power of the country.

The king, though professedly an autocrat, was yet completely under their sway. Themselves skilled in the arts and sciences of their day, beyond any other of the people of the East, they carefully retained in their own order, the secrets by which they had gained and maintained their power, yet directed the education of the masses, so as to qualify them for deeds of warlike prowess, and for such civil duties and artisan pursuits as they chose to commit to them.

In physical training, they seem to have excelled all the other oriental nations; allowing even to the future warriors but a meagre fare, and requiring of them a gymnastic discipline, which made them, at that period, very formidable; they required of all classes the strictest adherence to truth, and reckoned chastity and purity of soul among the highest virtues. The intellectual culture they allowed was but trifling, except to those who were to be physicians; these were taught that portion of the sciences which pertained to their profession, and were exhorted to practice the utmost care and caution in the art of healing.

At the time of Cyrus, and after his conquest of Babylon, the religion and the luxurious habits of the Babylonians were introduced, greatly to the injury and degradation of the Persians; but the picture which Xenophon draws of the Persian system of education, during the youth of Cyrus, is interesting.

The whole population (except, it would seem, the magi themselves and the poorer classes), were divided into four orders, according to their age: 1st, the boys under 17; 2d, the Ephebi, or youths from 17 to 27 years of age; 3d, the mature men from 27 to 52; 4th, the old men above 52 years of age. To each of these their proper apartments were assigned in the ελευθερα αγορα or public place of each town, far removed from the shops and markets. The boys, who commenced their training at the age of six years, lodged at home, and brought thence their meagre fare of bread and water-cresses, and a cup to draw water from the river, for their drink; they were taught equitation, the use of the bow and the javelin, and the importance of a truthful, noble, and courageous character; they were also taught the administration of justice, by the trial of any one of their own number who was in fault, by his peers; ingratitude, they were instructed, was the most heinous of crimes, and merited the severest of punishments. The young men (εφηβοι) lodged in the public apartments, were trained to military exercises, and were permitted, in turn, to accompany the king and nobles in hunting, but were restricted to half their usual fare, meagre as it was, while absent on their hunting expeditions; to which, however, they were permitted to add a portion of any game they might kill. They were also exercised in various public games. In case of war they formed a portion of the military force; the men of mature age constituted the reliable army of the country, and though engaged only a portion of the time in actual service, must, at all times, be ready to be called out. They did not, like the young men, carry the bow and javelin, but were clad in heavy armor, and bore a sword. The magistrates were selected from this class. The old men did not render military service, except in case of the invasion of their country, but remained at home and engaged in civil matters, forming a kind of jury for the administration of justice.

The privilege of this public instruction and training was only allowed to the sons of those who were able, from their wealth, to dispense with the services of their children. For the sons of the poor there was no education, except such as they might obtain at home. Female education was utterly neglected; the wife was the slave of her husband, and every morning must kneel at his feet, and ask, nine times, the question, "What do you wish that I should do?" and having received his reply, bowing humbly, she must withdraw and obey his commands.

The advent of Zartusht, or Zoroaster, the great Persian reformer, in the reign of Darius Hystaspes, was marked by a temporary reform of their religious system, which, under the influence of Babylonian manners, had sunk into licentiousness; but he appears, unlike Con-fut-see and Meng-tsee, the Chinese philosophers, to have attempted nothing in the way of education.

CHAPTER IV.

The Hebrews.—Beauty of their literature.—Evidence it affords of extensive acquaintance with natural science.—Instruction among the higher classes.—Learning of Solomon and some of his associates. —Education mostly confined to the family.—No schools, properly so called, among them, till near the Christian era.—Schools of the Rabbins.

THE *Hebrews* or *Israelites* next deserve our attention. Not naturally superior in intellectual ability to the nations around them, and for some centuries, owing to their pastoral and agricultural pursuits, possessing fewer opportunities of culture than the Egyptians and Babylonians, some of the race, nevertheless, attained to a remarkable degree of literary and scientific eminence. No literature of ancient times compares, for beauty or grandeur, with the Psalms, the book of Job, and portions of the prophetic books.

Solomon, though educated entirely in his own kingdom, was regarded by neighboring, and even remote nations, as a prodigy of learning. Several of the books of the Old Testament, and particularly Job, Psalms, and Proverbs, contain allusions which indicate a knowledge of science and the useful arts, greatly in advance of that possessed by adjacent nations.

The priestly class, as such, does not however seem to have possessed either the education or the influence which they had attained in Egypt or India. The wealthier classes cultivated science, and their children were taught by hired instructors; thus we find that the prophet Nathan, and Jehiel ben Hachmoni, were the governors or instructors of the sons of David. At the period of Solomon's accession to the throne, learning flourished more than at any previous, and perhaps more than at any subsequent period of the Israelitish history. In 1 Kings, iv. 31, we find the names of several eminent scholars of that time, viz.: "Ethan the Ezrahite, and Heman (possibly the eminent singer, so often referred to in the Psalms), Chalcol and Darda, the sons of Mahol."

Education among the Hebrews was not national, in the same sense as that of the Persians, or the Spartans; but rather conducted in the family, and, with the exception of the wealthier classes, seems to have been rather moral and æsthetic, than intellectual. Reading was not generally taught, at least in the earlier ages of their history; but the principles of the moral, and, to some extent, those of the ceremonial law, were communicated with great care and particularity from father to son. Obedience to parents was considered indispensable, while continued disobedience was punished by the death-penalty, as was also dissolute conduct on the part of the young. The use of the rod, by parents, to control and subdue refractory children, was not only allowed, but recommended; the history of the nation, with its miracles, and its fearful warnings, was very generally taught; and instrumental music, chanting, and improvisation, as well as dancing, which constituted a feature of their usual worship, formed a part of the course of instruction, with both sexes.

Architecture, sculpture, embroidery, and engraving, or chasing of the precious metals and gems, were also carried to a high degree of perfection.

The condition of woman, though low in the social scale, was still much higher than that of the surrounding nations; and in the later periods of their history, polygamy was entirely abandoned.

Unless we regard what are called by Jewish writers the schools of the prophets (for the early Hebrew has no term answering to our word *school*), as places of instruction, there was nothing like a public place of instruction in Palestine. That sacred chanting was practiced in their assemblies, and accompanied with the use of musical instruments, we know; that, as some writers conjecture, reading, writing, poetry, and the elements of philosophy and medicine were taught there, is less certain.

Near the commencement of the Christian era, and for a period of four or five hundred years after, there were schools, in Palestine and elsewhere, taught by the Rabbins, in which the instruction was confined to the laws of Moses, and the Rabbinical commentaries thereon, the Mischna, the Thora, and the Gemara—the larger portion of which the pupils were required to commit to memory. These commentaries were, for the most part, occupied with the most absurd and silly speculations concerning the sacred text, and their study was an injury rather than a benefit to the pupils.

We find nowhere any evidence that mathematics, beyond the mere rudiments of arithmetic, were taught among the Hebrews; and in their knowledge of astronomy they were far behind the Egyptians, the Babylonians, and the Greeks. Their men of learning must have cultivated some departments of physical science, for we are told of Solomon, 1 Kings, iv. 33, that "he spake of trees, from the cedar-tree that is in Lebanon, even unto the hyssop that springeth out of the wall; he spake also of beasts, and of fowl, and of creeping things, and of fishes." We find evidence also in the

Psalms, the Proverbs, and the book of Job, of critical research in the mineral as well as the vegetable and animal world.

CHAPTER V.

The Greeks.—Influence of their systems of education on other nations.—The Homeric period.—Ulysses, Achilles, and Patroclus.—The period of the Lawgivers.—LYCURGUS.—Brief biographical sketch.—The Spartan system.—More limited in its application than generally supposed.—SOLON.—Peculiarities of his system.—Instruction confined to the higher classes, and forbidden to slaves and women, except courtesans.—PYTHAGORAS.—His extensive travels.—The philosophic character of his instructions.—His course exoteric and esoteric.—General view of his system.—Its exemplification in some of his followers.

WE come next to speak of the educational systems of a people whose influence is felt on the intellects of all civilized nations, even to the present day. GREECE has perhaps exerted more sway, by her literature, over the minds of men in the two thousand years since her decadence, than in the ages when, in intellectual culture and in physical bravery, she stood first among the nations.

Her educational condition may perhaps be better understood, by a brief review of it at four periods. The *Homeric period*, or, as it is usually called, the *heroic age*, has so much of fable mixed with fact in its traditions, that it is only by incidental allusions in Homer and Hesiod, that we can discover what was the real intellectual condition of the people. There would seem to have been little answering to our notion of a school, existing during this period, unless the gatherings for chanting the Orphic hymns and other ascriptions of praise to the gods can be so regarded.

The art of healing was taught by the Asclepiades, and there were also schools of medicine (so called) at Crotona, a Greek colony in Italy, at Cneidus in Crete, and at Rhodes ; but the medical knowledge was scanty, and mostly confined to hygienic precepts. The education must have been mostly domestic, and probably did not include a knowledge of reading, as it is doubtful if letters were then known. Severe physical training, the government of the passions, knowledge of the world and of men, and reverence for the gods, seem to have been the principal subjects of instruction.

Natural science had made some progress

among a people so inquiring as the Greeks, and they had learned to recognize some of the heavenly bodies which glittered in their azure skies. Ulysses, who seems to have been Homer's ideal of a wise man, has drawn his knowledge from observation and experience.

Achilles and Patroclus had a special instructor or tutor; Hector's education, however attained, was such as to make him a model of noble manly valor, and of domestic virtue. The education of women was not wholly neglected. They were skilled in household duties, in embroidery; and some of them, like Penelope, Arete, and Nausikaa, were so intelligent as to fascinate, by their conversation, the heroes of their time.

Leaving this mythic age, we come to a period when history, though still occasionally beclouded by fable, gives us more light. The period of Lycurgus, of Solon, and of Pythagoras, embracing more than 250 years of Grecian history, viz.: from 776 B. C., to 520 B. C., may be regarded as the second stage of education in Greece.

The exact date of the birth of Lycurgus, as well as many facts in his history, are matters of uncertainty. The best accredited narratives make him a descendant of the Heraclidæ, the royal family of Sparta. He saved the kingdom for his infant nephew Charilaus, against the wiles of the queen-regent; and having, in consequence, incurred her enmity, he absented himself for many years, studying in foreign lands the laws and systems of government of the most civilized nations. At length, he returned, and found the State in confusion, and all parties soliciting his aid and counsel. Consulting the Delphic oracle, and receiving a favorable reply, he at once commenced, with the approbation of the king, a reform in the government. He issued a set of ordinances called *Rhetra*, by which he effected a total revolution in the political and military organization of the people, and in their social and domestic life.

The details of these ordinances it does not belong to our plan to give, except so far as they relate to education. It was the central idea of his system of education, that the child was the property, not of its parents, but of the State. The officers of the State must inspect it at its birth, and if sickly, or deformed, it was not permitted to live.

It was consigned to its parents, till its seventh year, to be brought up for the State; at that age, it was placed under the care of teachers, appointed by the government, fed on the most scanty and meager fare, to which, however, what could be obtained by hunting, and by theft, was added—if the theft was discovered it was severely punished. The physical instruction consisted of gymnastic exercises, sham fights, wrestling, and annual scourging, under which it was discreditable to utter any complaint, and many died under the scourge. The intellectual culture was very slight, consisting mainly in some rudimentary knowledge of arithmetic, in the practice of brevity and condensation in the expression of their thoughts—whence our word *laconic* is derived—and in some slight knowledge of astronomy. The moral culture consisted in the inculcation of truthfulness, the government of the passions, and reverence for the gods.

Females received substantially the same education as males; the object being to produce the most perfect and vigorous physical development: and hence the Spartan women were, in character and position, very much superior to the other women of Greece. This discipline was continued not only to manhood, but to middle age. It produced a nation of remarkable physical power and energy, warlike, and ready for any conflict; but it ignored all refinement, all esthetic culture, and all scientific attainment.

The proportion of the Lacedemonian population subjected to this discipline, was, however, much smaller than is generally supposed. The Spartans, though the dominant race, were by no means so numerous as the Penœci, who formed the farming population; or the Helots, who were, like the Russian serfs, in a condition of slavery, or rather villanage;—yet the system of discipline was confined to the Spartans, who numbered not more than 9000, and even these, unless able to furnish their proportion to the *Syssitia*, or public mess, were not admitted to the privileges of the system.

Solon (B. C. 638) was, like Lycurgus, a law-giver. He modified the severity of the penalties affixed to the violation of the laws of Athens, by his predecessor Draco; relieved the poor from slavery for debt, and materially changed the legislation relative to debtor and creditor. The popularity acquired by these measures was so great that he was called upon, by the great body of the people, to draw up a new code for the State, which he undertook, after some deliberation.

This code is mostly extant, and though there is nothing in it concerning education, yet the regulations existing at Athens, while the laws of Solon were in force, would seem to justify the assertions of later Greek writers, that he had made enactments on this subject also.

The system of Athenian education recognized intellectual culture, as equally necessary with physical training. The State had an interest in the education of its youth; and every citizen, under a severe penalty, was required to teach his son to read and to swim; he was also to teach him some occupation, and if he neglected to do this, the son was free from the obligation to support and care for him in his old age. But aside from these general enactments, there was a minutely detailed system of education prescribed for the children of Athenian citizens. Till their seventh year, they were under the care of their parents. At that age, they were sent to school, being accompanied always by the παιδαγωγος, who was generally a faithful slave, or friend of the family. The school was supported by the State, and its teachers were of two grades, the γραμματιότης or elementary teacher, who gave instruction in the alphabet, spelling, and writing; and the γραμματικος or κριτικος, who taught his pupils to commit and recite, or declaim, the finest passages of the Greek poets and historians, which he explained and criticised, and also gave instruction in poetical composition, music, eloquence, and the principles of the fine arts. Penmanship and a graceful elocution were studies to which especial attention was directed.

Parents were allowed to direct the order in which their children should take up the different studies. When the youth had arrived at manhood, he was taught, if he chose to study them, ethics, dialectics, politics, and mythology. Mathematics were not much taught at Athens, at least at this period. In this course of instruction, the children of the poor and the slaves were not allowed to participate, nor were female children allowed any instruction, except such as they might receive at home.

The condition of the female sex, except the abandoned portion of it, at Athens was pitiable; secluded from society and from intellectual improvement, their lives must have been gloomy, dull, and hopeless. To the courtesan, on the contrary, opportunities of education and culture were granted, and the learning and eloquence of some of these not only enabled them to rule the leaders of the

State, but gave them a reputation which has come down to our own times.

Pythagoras, born at Samos 604 B. C., was the most accomplished scholar and profoundest thinker of his day. The pupil of Anaximander and Thales, he subsequently spent many years in Egypt and other Oriental countries, where he acquired the learning of the priests, and the sciences in which Egypt at that time was pre-eminent. Returning thence, he visited the States of Greece, familiarized himself with the systems of government and education of Lycurgus and Solon, and finally settled at Crotona in Italy, one of the principal cities of the Greek colony, then known as Magna Græcia. Here he was received with great honors, the people being more intelligent than those of most of the Greek cities; and though he refused all direct participation in the government, yet, through his own influence and that of a secret association of three hundred which he formed, he controlled and molded their laws and institutions.

He was the first of the Greek philosophers

who founded a school or sect, which survived him for several hundred years. Like that of the priests and philosophers of Egypt and India, his system of education was two-fold, *exoteric* and *esoteric;* but, unlike theirs, both were based on the same principle, and the latter was but the more perfect development of the former. No previous philosopher had attained to such wide, grand, and comprehensive views as those which he enunciated, and none had ever propagated them by similar means.

With far greater learning, he yet resembled, in the vastness of his conceptions, his knowledge of human nature and its springs of action, and his power of controlling mind, Ignatius Loyola, more nearly than any man of ancient or modern times. The foundation of all science, in his view, lay in the harmony of the universe, and though his conceptions of the order, harmony, and music of the heavenly bodies seems to have been vague, yet it was sufficient to inspire his disciples with awe and interest.

Man, he contended, was but the universe in epitome, and since the *Kosmos* was ruled by the laws of harmony, it was becoming that in the affairs of man, the *Mikrokosmos*, there should be no discords. The attainment of this perfect harmony was the object of all education, and man could attain it by purification of the soul, by self-knowledge, and by devotion.

His idea of purification implied, not only the complete regulation of the life, the subduing of the passions, and the performance of good deeds, but also involved his doctrine of metempsychosis, or transmigration of souls. In self-knowledge was implied also a mastery of social knowledge, since society was but a larger self, and of the laws which govern the kosmos: and hence included science. Mathematics and music, in its comprehensive Grecian sense, as comprising not only melody, but poetical composition, the fine arts and eloquence, were among the necessary aids to this self-knowledge, and profound reflection was indispensable. He regulated the diet and exercise of his pupils with the most scrupulous care. Nor was he less observant of the morals and manners of his disciples; chastity and purity of thought and language, courtesy, benevolence, and self-sacrificing friendship were earnestly inculcated. The friendship of Damon and Pythias, so celebrated in ancient times, was cemented under his instruction, for they were his pupils.

His esoteric course, to which only his favorite disciples were admitted, though hedged in from the vulgar crowd by various rites and ceremonies, seems to have been only a more complete development of the exoteric course; extending the scientific training to a knowledge of astronomy, ethics, and the higher mathematics, and probably, also, to some departments of natural science. His instructions were not confined to his own sex, many of his female pupils afterward distinguishing themselves as authors.

CHAPTER VI.

The Greeks continued.—SOCRATES.—Eminently an educator.—His method.—The practical results more fully developed in the teachings of PLATO.—The theories of education of the latter as developed in his "Republic," his "Sophistes," and other works.—ARISTOTLE, the wisest of the Grecian teachers.—His "Natural History."—His "Politics."—Successors of Aristotle.—The schools of Athens and Alexandria.—Review of Greek education.

HAVING thus exhibited the intellectual condition of Sparta, Athens, and Magna Græcia, at a period less than 600 years before the Christian era, a condition more advanced, perhaps, than that of the rest of Greece, let us take another view of it, somewhat more than a century later, in the times of Socrates and Plato.

Socrates merits, perhaps more than any other man of ancient times, to be called an *educator*, in the literal sense of that term; for it was the great business of his public life to *draw out*, or educe truth, by questionings and analogies. Born 469 B. C., of humble parentage, rough and extremely unprepossessing in his appearance, and wearying the self-satisfied and aristocratic Athenians by the pertinacity his questions, he yet exerted a more powerful influence on the intellect, not only of Greece, but of the world, than any man who had preceded him.

He never assumed the badge of a teacher; never gathered his disciples about him, to lecture to them, as did the other philosophers of Greece; but always professing ignorance, made inquiries of any one, high or low, who would answer them, and always, in the end, discomfited them in argument by his dexterous questionings. Yet, though by his efforts the power of the Sophists, whose delusive theories had so long enchained the Greek intellect, was broken, and the foundations laid for a purer worship and a more earnest inquiry after truth in religion and science instituted, we shall find the practical results of his labors, in relation to education, more fully developed in the career and writings of his disciple, Plato, than in what of tradition has descended to our times concerning his own teachings.

Plato, born at Athens, 429 B. C., was a descendant of Solon and of Codrus. At the age of twenty he became a follower of Socrates, whose instruction he enjoyed for ten years. After the death of his friend and master, he traveled extensively, and subsequently gathered round him a body of disciples, to whom, in the gardens of Academia, he expounded the views and principles of his master, as well as those which his own grand and lofty intellect had wrought out. In his "*Republic*" and in his "*Laws*," he lays down his theory of education, a theory probably never fully reduced to practice, but which exerted a powerful influence on his nation for centuries.

During the eighteen or twenty years of his absence from Athens, he had visited Egypt and Persia, and studied attentively their systems of education and religious culture; he had also mastered, in detail, the laws and institutions of Lycurgus at Sparta, and observed the results of more than two hundred and fifty years' experience under them.

We find traces of the effect of these studies, in his scheme of a republic. Like Lycurgus, he regarded the children as the property of the State, and even recommended a community of wives, that there might be no impediment to the exercise of the parental power over them by the State, and that the physical beauty and vigor of the children might be increased. He opposed all education, except in their particular trades and in subjection to the laws, to the artisan and laboring classes; while he would have the military class very thoroughly trained. This training he would have commenced as early as the third year, for he believed infancy the most important period of human life, inasmuch as the impressions then made were never effaced.

Regarding a good teacher as one of the most essential conditions for the formation of good pupils, he lays down rules, in his "*Sophistes*," for distinguishing between a good and a bad teacher; and he recommends to those in power to exercise the utmost scrutiny and care in the selection of instructors, who were to be paid by the State. Plato could not, with his Greek notions of physical training, avoid giving great prominence to gymnastic exercises as a means of education, but he abated much of the Spartan severity both of exercise and diet, still retaining, however, sufficient to maintain the body in health and vigor.

To temper its tendency to make the man hard, harsh, and ferocious in his nature, he would have him pursue musical culture in connection with gymnastics. We have already explained the sense in which the Greeks used the word *music*, as implying all those studies which, in their mythology, were assigned to the care of the nine Muses. Plato seems, however, to have laid more stress on music proper than any of his predecessors had done, and to have cultivated it to a higher degree of perfection.

For the intellectual culture of his pupils, he recommended the thorough study of arithmetic, geometry, and astronomy; and if they would attain to eminence, philosophy also, as the sublimest of all intellectual pursuits. He would not, of course, neglect rhetoric, declamation, and the art of poetical composition, nor the principles of taste, which were indispensable in Athenian society. Moral culture was also a subject of consideration with him, and he urges, in strong terms, the necessity of reverence for the gods, respect for parents, obedience to the laws, and chastity and purity of life.

The "foremost man of all the Greeks," however, in general learning, in genius, and in his devotion to education, was ARISTOTLE. Born at Stageira, a city of Thrace, 384 B. C., of intelligent and noble parentage, his father Nicomachus being an eminent physician and author, and the friend of Amyntas II., king of Macedonia, the young Aristotle started in life with more external advantages than any of his predecessors, and his keen perceptions and vivacious temperament enabled him, under the genial training of his father, early to acquire knowledge. After his father's death, which occurred while he was yet a child, he was instructed by one Proxenus, a friend of his father, then residing at Stageira. At the age of seventeen he repaired to Athens, drawn thither by the fame of its eminent teachers, and especially of Plato, then in the maturity of his great powers.

About the time of his arrival there, Plato sailed for Sicily, where he remained for three years. Aristotle, nevertheless, improved this period, by studying under the eminent teachers still remaining at Athens; and on Plato's return, he at once became his pupil. His mental activity caused Plato soon to distinguish him as the *mind* (νους) of his school, and of the many brilliant intellects gathered there from all the adjacent countries, no one seems seriously to have contested the palm with him. Fond of teaching, he probably had some pupils for a time in Athens before Philip of Macedon placed his son, afterward Alexander the Great, under his charge. For four years he labored zealously to make his illustrious pupil eminent in science, as he afterward became in arms; and the impress of his teachings was visible in many incidents of Alexander's subsequent career.

He ever reverenced his instructor, and lavished on him abundant wealth and facilities for the prosecution of his favorite study of natural history. Released from his charge as tutor, by the death of Philip and the succession of Alexander to the throne of Macedon, Aristotle returned to Athens, and there established a school, called the Lyceum, from its neighborhood to the temple of Apollo Lyceius. Here, for thirteen years, he taught two classes daily, walking in the garden or grove, and lecturing as he walked, whence he and his disciples received the name of *Peripatetics.*

His morning lecture was addressed to the more advanced of his pupils, and treated of dialectics, physical science, and the more profound topics of philosophy; his afternoon lectures or walks were addressed to a larger company, and in these he discussed political, ethical, and rhetorical questions. His vast learning brought to his school eminent men from every part of the then known world, and the influence of his philosophy has come down even to our own times, while the discoveries of our most eminent naturalists are constantly confirming the observations made by the Greek philosopher 2200 years ago.

His "*Politics*" includes a treatise on education, only a part of which is preserved. This work, unlike the Republic of Plato, is not a description of a theoretic State, but an elaborate discussion of the principles of government.

He may be justly regarded as the first really scientific teacher of youth, and his educational essay is evidently a summary of his own observation and experience. He extended, somewhat, the topics of study, and though he enumerates but four principal branches as necessary—viz.: gymnastics, music, grammar, or the study of language, and the arts of design—it is evident that he included in these more than we now do. Geography, in which Thales and Anaximander had made some progress, under the plastic hands of Aristotle assumed the form of a science.

Natural history, through his extensive observations and his inductive reasoning, became a science of fair proportions. Logic he invented, and his use of the syllogism was the commencement of a new era in the art of reasoning. Mathematics he regarded as of great importance for a thorough education, and a knowledge of politics, or the science of government, as necessary to the intelligent citizen. He urged the right of woman to education, but asserted that the slaves should not be taught any thing beyond obedience to their masters.

The influence of Aristotle's lectures and works upon his followers and their pupils, for many of them taught in public, led to a still greater enlargement of the bounds of science, and to the systemization of a complete course of instruction, known, some three centuries after his time, as the *εγκυκλια παιδεύματα*, from whence comes our word *encyclopedia.*

This "circle of sciences" consisted, in the

Alexandrian schools, at the commencement of the Christian era, of the seven liberal arts—grammar, rhetoric, dialectics, arithmetic, geometry, astronomy, and music. But rhetoric was also cultivated aside from the other studies.

Athens, from the time of Plato and Aristotle, became the resort of those who sought a superior education, and though the morals and manners of its people greatly degenerated, and its professors of philosophy and science taught for the sake of fees, a practice which Socrates, Plato, and Aristotle denounced; and though they too often sought popularity by pandering to corrupt tastes, yet, for five or six centuries, it maintained its pre-eminence.

About a hundred years after the death of Aristotle, Alexandria began to be its most formidable rival; and during the sway of the Ptolemaic dynasty, the noble libraries and the high repute of the grammarians, or professors in its schools, attracted almost as many youth from abroad as Athens. The character of the teaching, in both cities, was far inferior to that of the time of Aristotle. The logic and dialectics which he taught, and which he intended as aids in the exercise of the reasoning faculties, had been perverted to the consideration of silly quibbles; and volumes were written and months of argument passed, in the discussion of questions which, when decided, added nothing to the sum of human knowledge. For five centuries no man stood forth among this host of philosophers and dialecticians, to make any valuable additions to science or to philosophy.

In the review of Greek education, we find that it was, from the first, considered the affair of the State; that, for the most part, the system of education was designed to fit men for military life, though, in the later periods, reference was also had to political life; that generally, women, except the most abandoned, were denied its privileges; that it was only the children of the aristocracy, those who could live without labor, who received its advantages; that artisans, laborers, and the serfs and slaves were rigorously forbidden all participation in it; that, in the earlier ages, the education was physical and moral, rather than intellectual, while, in the later ages, moral culture was neglected, and intellectual education usurped its place; that the favorite studies of the Greeks were rather rhetoric, dialectics, ethics, metaphysics, and so much of the mathematics as would aid them in becoming skillful reasoners and ready debaters, than the pursuit of natural or high mathematical science; that while they understood their own language well, they had no taste for linguistics in general, regarding other nations as barbarians, and their languages as imperfect.

CHAPTER VII.

THE ROMANS.—Early education mainly moral and physical.—Introduction of Greek instruction.—Education under the Empire.—Tendencies of the Roman less intellectual than those of the Greek. —Female education not general.—Quintilian.—Varro.—The orphan schools of Antoninus Pius.—The Druids.—Little known of their system of education.

THE ROMANS seem never to have entertained the idea that it was the duty of the State to educate the children of its citizens. In the early periods of their history, education was entirely domestic, and the amount of intellectual culture was very scanty. The father possessed absolute power over his family, even to the taking of life; but this power, though exercised with considerable severity and sternness, seems to have been seldom abused. The father was regarded with reverence and respect, seldom, perhaps, with very strong affection, for the Latin word *pietas*, which expressed the emotion of the dutiful child to his parent, can hardly be thought to imply much of love. Physical training was not neglected, and the moral culture was probably of a higher character than that of any other nation, with the possible exception of the Hebrews.

The ability to read and write were rare acquirements, and these, with perhaps some knowledge of arithmetic, were only imparted to a few of the children of patrician parents. The legend of Virginia relates that "she was going to her school in the tabernæ of the forum," when the client of Appius Claudius seized her; but as there is no other evidence of the existence of a school in the forum, and especially for girls, till several centuries later, we must consider this as an embellishment, added to the story by a later hand.

That writing was but little known or practiced, and that the early history of Rome was (except some brief annals which were burned by the Gauls, 390 B. C.) mostly transmitted by oral tradition, is distinctly testified by Livy. It was not until the Romans had conquered the Italian cities settled by Greek colonies, such as Tarentum, Crotona, and Syracuse, that the literature, the philosophy, and the educational systems of Greece began to exert an influence on them.

After that period, Greek teachers and philosophers came to Rome in crowds; and, though Cato the Censor and others, dreading their influence, attempted to drive them from the city, they had obtained too strong a foothold to be dislodged. The Greek literature was adopted almost without modification, and no Roman scholar was ignorant of it. The philosophy was not so readily received, and but for the education of the young Romans in Athens, would hardly have established itself; for the Roman was harder, coarser, and less susceptible of esthetic culture than the Greek; he delighted more in blood, and less in beauty; more in facts, and less in speculation; more in the real, and less in the ideal. It was not, therefore, till the best traits of his character were lost, in the luxury and sensuality of the later years of the republic, that he began to take kindly to the rhetoric, the dialectics, and the philosophy of the Greeks, and, indeed, the descendants of the old Romans never fairly mastered them.

The distinguished teachers, as well as the celebrated writers, of Rome were, for the most part, either natives of the colonies or provinces, or freedmen, who had once been the slaves of the wealthy. Schools for instruction in grammar, arithmetic, geometry, and elocution, existed in Rome for more than a hundred years before the Christian era, and some of the teachers attained eminence; but these schools were attended only by the children of the wealthy, and the young men went to Athens, Rhodes, or Alexandria, to finish their education.

The masses were not educated, or intelligent; they took little interest in the dramatic representations which were translated from the Greek, and which possessed extraordinary merit; if an author attempted to exhibit an original drama, he was persecuted and abused, until he abandoned the effort in disgust; the only public exhibitions which attracted the attention and received the plaudits of the populace, were the pantomimes, whose principal recommendation was their indecency, and the gladiatorial shows, where cruelty was added to the indecency.

A few of her eminent men distinguished themselves as orators, poets, and historians, and some of these, like Tacitus and Sallust, developed the power of the language for vigorous and condensed expression; but most, like Cicero, Cæsar, Virgil, and Horace, betray, unconsciously perhaps, but yet clearly, that they are indebted to the Greek poets and orators for many of their thoughts, and even for their forms of expression. The later poets differ from the Greek poets, but only in the unblushing license and obscenity of their language, which would have rendered their writings highly offensive to the esthetic sense of the Greeks.

In one particular, however, the Romans might justly claim superiority over the other nations of the world. Their architecture was wonderful for its solidity and grace, and they filled not Rome only, but the world, at least so much of it as they subdued and colonized, with their enduring structures. The traveler of to-day, whether he visit northern Africa, far on toward the confines of the desert, England, France, Spain, Germany, southern Russia, Turkey, or the cities of Asia Minor, Palestine, or Arabia, finds everywhere dwellings, castles, aqueducts, or bridges, which have defied alike the erosions of time, the shock of earthquakes, and the desolating progress of successive armies of invaders. The perfection and durability of these structures necessarily imply a high degree of mathematical and geometrical knowledge, and hence indicate that the architects, if not the artisans, who erected them, must have been well-educated.

The period between the commencement of the Christian era and the conversion of Constantine, during which Rome was yet pagan, though a period of moral degradation, was one in which literature and intellectual culture flourished, more than at any previous time, in the Roman Empire. Augustus and his minister Mæcenas were patrons of literature and promoters of education. To the right of citizenship, which Julius Cæsar had conferred on foreign grammarians and other teachers, as well as physicians, who settled at Rome, Augustus added their exoneration from public offices and other occupations.

During his administration, also, several new schools, of high repute, were established in the the provinces, to which young men flocked in great numbers; such were Mytilene, Massilia (now Marseilles), and Corduba in Spain. The first institution resembling a college, in the Roman Empire, was founded by Vespasian (A. D. 69–79), who appointed Quintilian a public professor of eloquence, giving him a salary from the public funds, and also employed, with salaries, several other professors of rhetoric.

What Vespasian originated, Adrian (A. D. 117–138), carried out to completion; founding in the capital an institution, called the Athenæum, and appointing a corps of professors of grammar, as well as rhetoric, with respectable salaries. Antoninus Pius, his successor (A. D. 138–161), not only added a professorship of philosophy to the Athenæum, but established a similar institution in the most important cities of the Empire. The course pursued by the professors was, according to the testimony of Suetonius, Gellius, Quintilian, and others, to expound the writings of Cicero and the poems of Virgil, Horace, Statius, &c., in the Latin language, and of the principal Greek authors in the Greek. The grammarians certified, at stated times, the progress made by their pupils, urging them forward by the influence of emulation, and still more by the use of the rod.

Among the Roman writers on education, we may mention M. Terentius Varro, "the most learned man in Rome," and one of her most voluminous writers. He was born 116 B. C., and died about 27 B. C. Of his work, entitled "*Capys, aut de liberis educandis*," only a few fragments now remain. Cicero treats of education, incidentally, in his "*De Officiis*." M.

Fabius Quinctilianus, or, as he is usually called, Quintilian, the most celebrated rhetorician of his age (A. D. 42–120), also speaks, at length, of the existing systems of education, and suggests improvements, in the first book of his "*Institutio Oratoria*," which is still extant.

Antoninus Pius (A. D. 138–161) was the first Roman monarch, and probably the first pagan monarch, who ever established a school for orphans. At the death of his wife, Annia Faustina (A. D. 138), to whom, notwithstanding her reputed ill-conduct, he was tenderly attached, he established a school for orphan and foundling girls, whom he named "*Puellæ Faustinianæ.*" The success of this seems to have incited him to establish similar schools for both sexes, which were called "*Pueri et Puellæ Alimentarii.*" Five medals now in existence, of dates corresponding to 141, 149, 151, 160, and 161, A. D., testify to the organization of these schools in different cities.

Several centuries before the Christian era, there existed in the British islands a form of civilization, and an intellectual and religious culture, known as Druidism, bearing marks of foreign derivation, yet exerting a powerful influence on the people. It was apparently of Grecian or Oriental origin, as the educated classes used the Greek language, while its religious forms and ceremonies indicated an affinity with Egypt or India. But few reliable data of this religious system have been transmitted to our time, for the Roman culture and worship almost entirely effaced it from the memories of the people, and the introduction of new nations, Romans, Saxons, Danes, and Normans, have obliterated the little that remained.

We know, however, that its chief seat was on the island of Mona, or Anglesey; that the priestly and legislative power were held by the same persons; that they gave instruction, usually, in the open air, and under the wide-spreading boughs of an oak (a tree which they held sacred), to the youth of the wealthier and priestly classes, in reading, writing, arithmetic, geography, the mysteries of nature, and the peculiar tenets of their religious system.

With these instructions something of mystery was always mingled; many of them were never committed to writing; and there was, for those who were intended for the Druidical priesthood, an esoteric course, like the Brahminical instruction of India. This Druidical system had also pervaded, to some extent, the north of Europe, though the daring and adventurous spirit, and the exuberance of animal life, in the Scandinavian races, had modified its traditions, and while they added to their fierceness, violence, and cruelty, had almost ignored their intellectual characteristics.

CHAPTER VIII.

Education among the Arabs and Saracens.—Period prior to Mohammed.—Influence of Mohammed.—The Ommiades and Abassides.—The translation of Aristotle.—Spain, the principal seat of Saracen learning.—Its extent.—Mexican provision for education.—The Calmecac.—Picture writing.—Their calendar.—The Council of Music and its duties.—Mexican poetry.—The Peruvians.—Their intellectual culture less extensive than the Mexican.—The *Quipu*.—The ballads of the *haravecs*.—Agriculture among the Peruvians.

BEFORE speaking of education as influenced by Christianity, we must give a brief account of its progress among the Arabs, under the sway of Mohammed and his successors; and also among the Mexicans and Peruvians, where, as among the nations already noticed, it was not modified by the influence of Christianity.

The Arabs, prior to the advent of Mohammed, were not distinguished for intellectual culture; those of them who dwelt in towns had attained to about the same amount of education with the early Hebrews; those who were nomadic had even less; the instruction was almost wholly domestic, and mainly physical and moral.

Few among them could read, and fewer still could write; yet the poetical element was highly developed, and the family, tribal, and national history were embalmed in a rude but impassioned poetry, which young and old had committed to memory; every tribe, indeed almost every section of a tribe, had its bard, who was ever a welcome and honored guest, and for whom, even in times of hunger and privation, the best was always reserved; these bards acted, in some sense, as the schoolmasters of the nation. The pilgrimages to Mecca, where the Kaaba, or sacred black stone (an aerolite, probably), which was fabled to have descended from heaven, rested, also had their share in the education of the people, bringing together, as they did, pilgrims from every part of Arabia, and from adjacent countries.

The state of morals among the Arabs, at this period, was much higher than that of the nations around them. They, of all the Orientals, were monogamists, and though the social rank of woman was not so high as with us, it was higher than elsewhere in the east. They were, perhaps, idolaters, but their pantheon was small, and confined to the inferior deities; and in their social character, hospitality, ardent friendship, a high sense of honor, and indomitable courage were marked traits.

Mohammed, born about A. D. 570, and, after his fortieth year, professing to be divinely inspired, wrought a most wonderful change in the character of these wild descendants of Ishmael. Whether we regard him as an enthusiast, a fanatic, or a deceiver, we can not fail to see that his system possessed many features wonderfully attractive to a people like the Arabs, and that once received by them as a divine revelation, it must necessarily modify their whole subsequent history. It is foreign to our purpose to consider the Koran in any other relation than that of its bearing upon education.

We find Mohammed enjoining it as a sacred duty upon his followers to read the Koran;

the necessity and advantages (spiritual as well as temporal) of learning are prominent topics in it; yet the social position of woman was lowered, polygamy permitted and practiced by the prophet himself, and the relation of parent and child debased rather than honored. Idolatry was forbidden, but pilgrimages to Mecca and Medina, thenceforth to be sacred shrines, from their connection with the prophet, allowed and enjoined.

A new impulse, a fresh start, was given to the Arabic mind, which made it for the next six centuries the leading intellect of the world. But though this wondrous intellectual advancement, in a people who had hitherto taken no prominent part in the world's civilization, resulted from the change effected by the introduction of his professed revelations, yet, in the subsequent mental development of that people, very little is due to Mohammed's influence. The first demonstration of the new religion was a bloody conflict; for almost a century the Khalifs extended the empire of their faith by the sword, fighting as men always do who have a strong, earnest conviction, a tangible faith, to fight for, and conquering, of course.

It was not till this warlike fervor had passed away, and the successors of the prophet saw the whole of Arabia, Palestine, Persia, a great part of India, Egypt, and northern Africa subjected to the faith of Islam, that they settled down quietly to the more intellectual development of their creed.

The children were to be taught the Koran, and, as if by magic, thousands of schools were opened to instruct them in reading; serious differences of opinion had arisen in relation to the proper interpretation of the sacred book, and schools of learning, whose ultimate object was to throw light upon the dark places in it, were organized.

The profound investigations deemed necessary for this purpose led to the introduction of other sciences and to the study of the Greek writers, some of whose works had been translated into the Syrian tongue by the Nestorians, and perhaps also into Arabic, in the fifth century; Aristotle began to be a familiar author with learned Saracens, and Arabic literature was enriched with numberless works in every department of science.

Libraries were found to be indispensable, and the Ommiade and Abasside Khalifs, lovers and patrons of learning, collected at Bagdad, at Damascus, and other cities of the East, books in such quantities as seem to us, even with modern facilities for their multiplication, almost fabulous.

In mathematics, they invented algebra; in medicine, they made greater progress than had been attained since the days of Hippocrates; in their researches in alchemy, they laid the foundations of chemical science; in astronomy, they made greater discoveries in the starry heavens, in the planetary systems, and in the motions of the earth and the sun, than all who had gone before them. There is reason to believe that they were not ignorant of the use of the telescope, and even their astrological researches led to some important progress in astronomical science. To them are we indebted for bringing into use our admirable system of numerals; and if, as some pretend, they received the first hint of it in India, they were certainly the first to disseminate it through Europe.

During the administration of Almansor, Haroun Al-Raschid, and Mamoun, grammatical studies, poetry, philosophy, jurisprudence, medicine, astronomy, mathematics, natural science, and magic were taught in their schools; and besides the schools at Bagdad and Damascus, new ones were founded, and attained a high reputation, at Basra, Kufa, Aleppo, Bokhara, and other large cities, while the seminaries of the Jews and Christians at Berytus, Nisibis, Antioch, and Edessa, were not only tolerated, but encouraged.

It was in Spain, however, that the highest development of the Saracenic intellectual culture took place, or, at least, our knowledge of its development there is more full than elsewhere. The Moors, under the aggressive impulse of their new faith, had crossed the Straits of Gibraltar, about the commencement of the eighth century, swept over the fertile lands of Spain almost without resistance, and, under the leadership of the brave and bold Abd-el-Malek, pushed forward to subdue France also; but their onward progress was stayed by Charles Martel, who, by his great victory over them in A. D. 732, on the banks of the Loire, caused the tide of invasion to roll back upon itself.

For nearly seven centuries the Moslem power continued to prevail in Spain, waning indeed and restricted in its territory toward the last, and almost always engaged in war with the Christian nations which claimed Spain as their lawful heritage, and their allies in the adjacent nations. Yet human history has hardly recorded elsewhere so brilliant a career as that of the Saracens in Spain.

The plains, the valleys, and the hillsides were covered with palaces and costly dwellings, in the light and graceful styles of Moorish architecture. Poetry and the fine arts flourished; the courts of the Moorish monarchs were the resort of eminent scholars; and over the whole land, schools and universities, with rich endowments, able professors, and large and valuable libraries, had sprung up under the fostering care of the government. Hakem II. (796–822), Almanzor, Ab-der-Rahman II., and Ab-der-Rahman III. were the noblest patrons of science among the Moorish kings. During the reign of the last-named king, about 940 A. D., there were in in existence seventeen universities, the most renowned of which was Cordova (which even in Roman times had been distinguished as a seat of literature), and sixty-six public libraries, of which that at Cordova alone contained six hundred thousand volumes. Notwithstanding the contempt with which the Koran treated women, female education was not neglected in Spain, and many of the most eminent poetical writers of the nation were of the gentler sex. All the advantages of the public seminaries were equally free to them, and the devoirs paid by the chivalric knights to the ladies of their choice were as often in homage to their high intellectual endowments as to the charms of their beauty and virtue.

The universities of Toledo, Salamanca, and Seville, though inferior in renown to Cordova, were yet celebrated all over Europe; and the African cities of Kairwan, Tunis, Fessan, and Algiers could also boast of their high-schools.

Indeed, whatever of civilization and education has penetrated beyond the desert into Negroland and the adjacent countries, can be traced directly to Moorish invasion and Mohammedan learning. Egypt, too, under the sway of the Khalifs, regained her old renown, and schools and colleges again testified to her zeal for education.

The brilliant results of the early ages of Moslem sway have vanished: the poets, philosophers, mathematicians, astrologers, and alchemists of the times of the Abassides are gone, and have left no successors to fill their places; and though, in all the Mohammedan cities, schools for boys are still maintained, and the higher studies are prosecuted to some extent, the zeal that once animated the teachers, the profound learning, and the literary and scientific attainments which made them the most accomplished nation of the world, are passed away.

The intellectual condition of the MEXICANS and PERUVIANS, at the date of their discovery by Europeans, has been a theme of general surprise. We find among them a clumsy, hieroglyphical language, co-existing with mathematical attainments of a high order, and a general mental culture superior to that of most of the nations of Europe two centuries earlier; the most revolting rites and human sacrifices, with a refinement of manners, and sublimity in the forms of worship, unparalleled among other idolatrous nations; a stern and strict system of morals, from which even the monarch, absolute as he was, could not depart with impunity.

The fascinating pages of Mr. Prescott's histories of Mexico and Peru, have given us a most graphic picture of the educational condition of these countries, and from them and other sources less widely known we are able to form a very complete conception of it.

In MEXICO, the children of both sexes, of

the higher and middle orders, were taught at the temples, the boys by the priests, the girls by the priestesses—for the sacerdotal function was exercised by both sexes. In these institutions the discipline and instruction were monastic; committing to memory religious chants, to be rehearsed at the festivals, feeding the sacred fires, and decorating the shrines of the gods with flowers were their principal duties. After a time they were transferred to a higher school, the *Calmecac*, where they learned the historical traditions of the country, the mysteries of hieroglyphics, the principles of government, and such branches of arithmetical, astronomical, and natural science as the priests were able to teach.

The girls were taught various feminine employments, and especially to weave and embroider rich coverings for the sacred altars. The moral discipline was rigid and severe, and the government of the schools was rather that of terror than love. For those who contemplated entering the priesthood there was a still higher education, in which an esoteric course of instruction was given. On their papyrus, prepared from the leaves of the maguey or American aloe, were inscribed by these young neophytes the history of the past, the poems and the liturgy of the nation, and the records of current events, in those suggestive hieroglyphics which seem to have been, to the initiated, but a kind of stenography, which implied far more than was written.

The books thus prepared were collected in large quantities in the larger cities of the empire, and, but for the ruthless barbarity of the conquerors, would have given us much fuller information of the history, habits, and manners of the races which had inhabited Mexico than we now possess. Of the several dialects spoken in Mexico, that of Tezcuco was the most polished and expressive, and its literature abounded in poetry and in eloquent and effective prose composition.

In mathematical science they had made remarkable progress. Their adjustment of the civil year to the actual revolution of the earth around the sun, one of the most difficult problems of science, was more perfect than that of the European astronomers, varying from the actual length only two minutes, nine second. Their system of chronology was simple, yet highly ingenious, and perfect for its purpose. They had invented the sun-dial, and, Lord Kingsborough thinks, from some carvings on rocks, the telescope. They also, as Sr. Gama has demonstrated, possessed the means of settling the hours of the day with precision, the periods of the solstices and equinoxes.

The admonitions of the father and mother to an Aztec maiden, on her coming to years of discretion, as preserved by Sahagun, show a tenderness and affection, as well as an elevated tone of morals, which speaks well for the character of the nation.

The education of the members of the royal family was very thorough, and, in addition to the branches usually taught in the *Calmecac*, comprehended the arts of working in metals, jewelry, and feather mosaic. Among the most eminent of the Mexican princes and philosophers was *Nezahualcoyotl*, a prince of pure character, great learning, and extraordinary genius, whose perceptions of religious truth seem to have been as accurate and sublime as those of Socrates and Plato, and whose patronage of learning is deserving of record. His hymns, or religious poems, have a lofty pathos and a pensive tenderness hardly equalled by any uninspired writings.

Among the extraordinary institutions of Mexico, one is deserving of notice in a history of education: the tribunal called the Council of Music, but whose object was the encouragement of science and art. All works on any science must be submitted to its censorship, before they could be made public. All the productions of art, and the nicer fabrics, were also subjected to its scrutiny. The professors in the various branches of science were obliged to pass an examination before it ere they entered on their duties, and the schools of the country were under its special supervision. On stated days, historical compositions and poems on moral or traditional topics were recited before it by their authors, and prizes awarded to the successful competitors.

In PERU there had been less intellectual progress. There was no written language, and the *quipu*, a fringe of cord about two feet long, of various colors, on which dates, amounts, and events were specified by means of knots, was their only substitute for written records. This was used more for arithmetical purposes, and as a system of mnemonics, than for any other purpose.

Education was withheld from the masses by royal injunction. Only the children of the Incas, and their descendants, could receive instruction. These, who formed the nobility of the nation, and were very numerous, were placed under the care of the *Amantas*, or wise men, who were the sole teachers of youth. The children were instructed in their national history, in the art of government, and in the peculiar rites of their religion. They also received some instruction in rhetoric, the art of elocution, the elements of arithmetic, and the understanding of the *quipus*.

The ballads of the *haravecs*, or national poets, which were mostly of an historical character, were also committed to memory by the youth, and chanted at the royal festivals. The government maintained theatrical exhibitions, in which both tragedies and comedies were performed; being, in this respect, in advance of the Mexicans, who had gone no further than pantomime. In astronomical knowledge they were inferior to the Aztecs, not being able to adjust so accurately the variation between the lunar and solar year. They had, however, learned to take azimuth observations, and had ascertained, very correctly, the times of the solstices and the period of the equinoxes. They knew some of the planets, but did not, like the Mexicans, understand the causes of eclipses.

In agricultural science they were far in advance of any other American race; with the methods of irrigation, draining, manuring, terracing steep hillsides, and the rotation of crops, they were familiar. They had made use of guano as a manure for centuries before the discovery of this continent, and along the sea-coast used the sardines, which were very abundant, for enriching their lands, in the same way that the menhaden or white-fish is used by our farmers on the seaboard. Their plow was a rude affair, it is true; but they managed to stir the soil more deeply with it, than their European successors did with an imported implement. They were also accomplished road-builders, and the great highway of the Incas from Quito to Cuzco, even in its present ruined state, exhibits an amount of engineering ability which would have done no discredit to a highly civilized nation.

In this brief sketch of the educational condition of the nations unaffected by Christianity, we can not fail to be impressed with the following facts: that education was universally considered as the privilege or perquisite of the higher classes alone; that it was generally regarded as the affair of the State, and its object was the preparation of the youth for a military, political, or priestly career; that the masses were purposely kept in the most abject ignorance, as thereby they were more readily controlled by the intelligent few; that in most countries the privilege of education was denied to the female sex, except in the case of those who were unchaste; and that the motives of religion, morality, or philanthropy had no influence in the promotion of intellectual culture. Let us now turn our attention to the character and progress of education when influenced and controlled by a new motive-power, Christianity.

CHAPTER IX.

EDUCATION SINCE THE CHRISTIAN ERA.—The character and influence of the teachings of Christ and of his apostles.—The influence of Christianity in modifying the family relation and the social and intellectual position of woman.—Testimony of Libanius.—Early Christian education mainly domestic.—School at Alexandria.—Pantænus.—Origen.—Schools at Cesarea.—At Antioch, Edessa, Rome, Carthage, &c.—The schools for Catechumens merely of a religious character.

WE have already seen how powerful was the influence exerted on the education of their several nations by Con-fut-see, Zartusht, Lycurgus, Pythagoras, Socrates, Plato, Aristotle, and Mohammed; yet none of these were capable of producing a tithe, or even a hundredth part, of the change in the controlling motives of men and nations which was the result of the teachings of the Founder of Christianity; there were radical differences in the character of their instruction and his: they dealt only with the words and outward conduct of their disciples; he, with the thoughts and intents of the heart: they recommended virtue from considerations of policy, and personal comfort and advantage; he, as a natural manifestation of a heart filled with love to God and to our fellow-men: they withheld knowledge from the poor, the lowly, the abject; he recognized it as the birthright of every son and daughter of Adam: they, for the most part, excluded woman from education, and from the social position which she was qualified by her Creator to adorn; he honored woman in all the relations of life, and opened wide the gates of instruction to her: they recommended no measures of philanthropic relief to the sick, the suffering, the infirm, or the enslaved; while he regarded the comfort, solace, and relief of these as a part of his special mission.

With principles differing so widely from those of all previous teachers and philosophers, it can not occasion surprise that the results of the predominance of his faith should have been such as to revolutionize all former systems of education; we can only wonder that the perversity, ignorance, and willfulness of man have, to such an extent, prevented their complete development.

During the three years of his public ministrations, Jesus was almost incessantly engaged in giving instruction. To the crowds which followed his footsteps he taught in parables, usually drawn from nature or from the customs and practices of the Jewish family—a method previously practiced by the Hebrew prophets, and to some extent by the pagan philosophers.

To his more immediate and intimate disciples these were explained and illustrated with more completeness than in his public discourses; to them, also, he more fully developed his plans, his purposes, and his doctrines; yet there was, in this special teaching, nothing analogous to the esoteric system of the Greek, Egyptian, and Hindoo philosophers and priests, for these instructions were only intended to qualify them to declare, with more clearness and accuracy, the truths which he had come to establish.

The high and sacred character which he

affixed to the marriage relation, the prohibition of polygamy, and of divorce except for a single cause, and the elevation of the social position of woman, taught both by precept and example; and the tenderness and love which he manifested for children, so different from the sternness of the Hebrew parents, and so incompatible with the gross and cruel selfishness which had led pagan philosophers to advise, and pagan parents to practice, the destruction of the feeble and infirm among their children—all demonstrated how radical a change of principle, in the position of woman and the education of children, he was to introduce.

Of his disciples and apostles, Luke and Paul were men of superior education; and while the one was the chronicler of the sayings and doings of his divine Master and of the early Church,—the other, by public disputation, by written argument, by oral instruction, and by his admirable letters, convinced his opponents, and taught the churches he had planted. In his writings, and those of the other apostles, we find frequent precepts on the education and training of children, designed to impress upon parents the modification, in their relations to their children, which their profession of Christianity had effected, and to enforce upon the young the duty of filial obedience from higher motives than those of fear.

The parental rule, under the Hebrew, the Greek, and the Roman laws, was one of extreme severity; the parent possessed the power even of putting his child to death, and fear, not love, was the predominant motive of action on the part of the child. The apostles sought to substitute the principle of mutual love, and the spirit of Christian tenderness and obedience, for this severity and fear, and they were successful.

In the first century of the Christian era, domestic education reached a higher point, in the families of the Christians, than it had ever previously attained. The children were not, perhaps, so conversant with Greek literature as some of their heathen neighbors, but their modesty, their courteous manners, their reverence for their parents, their knowledge of the Scriptures, and their general intelligence called forth the unwilling commendation of their enemies.

The purity and chastity, even in thought and conversation, of the Christian maidens, formed so marked a contrast with the general license indulged by the daughters of the pagans, that it elicited the encomiums even of the bitterest pagan writers. The high social position accorded to woman in the Christian system, had operated so favorably in drawing out the best points in her character, that the Christian mothers of the first centuries of the Christian era had no occasion to fear a comparison with the noble women of the heroic days of the Roman republic. The names of Anthusa, the mother of Chrysostom, of Nonna, the mother of Gregory Nazianzen, and of Monica, the mother of Augustine, will occur to many of our readers as justifying the exclamation of their bitter enemy, Libanius, "What wonderful women are these, of the Christian faith!"

The first school of high grade exclusively under Christian control, was that of the Catechists at Alexandria, said to have been founded by Pantænus, A. D. 181, and continued, after his death, by Clement, who, in his turn, was succeeded, A. D. 213, by Origen, and he by Heraclas. The object of this school was to qualify young men to become preachers; and besides the instruction in theology, mathematics, logic, rhetoric, natural philosophy, metaphysics, ethics, and astronomy were also taught. It continued in existence until about the middle of the fourth century, and perhaps even later.

As, however, it was impossible for all, or even the greater part, of those who entered the ministry to resort to Alexandria for instruction, it was customary with the more highly educated pastors and bishops to receive pupils into their own families, and instruct them in the profane sciences as well as in theology. The renown of the school at Alexandria was the more extraordinary from the fact that it was established at the period when the pagan school of Alexandria, founded by Ptolemy Soter, and sustained and endowed by his successors and the Roman emperors, was in the zenith of its reputation; having a noble library (the Museum), and a corps of the most renowned philosophers of that period among its professors. To its teachings many of the most eminent of the Christian preachers were indebted for their education.

Origen, whom we have named as one of the teachers of the school of Catechists, and who was, perhaps, the most eminent Christian scholar of his time, was banished from Alexandria in A. D. 231, and soon after established a similar school at Cesarea in Palestine, which attained to considerable distinction. Schools of the same character were established, a little later, at Antioch and at Edessa.

In the west, Christian schools were founded, as early as the beginning of the fourth century, in Rome, Carthage, Milan, Treves, Autun, Marseilles, and Lyons. Some writers have confounded with these the schools for Catechumens, which were held everywhere, and which were intended only to instruct the young and the ignorant in the elementary principles of Christian doctrine; but the two had no connection.

CHAPTER X.

Period of Constantine and his successors.—The Western Empire given over to barbarism.—Corruption of the Latin language.—CAPELLA.—Analysis of his *Satyricon*.—CASSIODORUS.—Worthlessness of his text-books.—Bishop Isidore of Seville.—Contents of his *Origines*.—This regarded as the most learned book of the dark ages.—The cathedral and monastic schools.—Meagerness of instruction in them.—Scarcity of parchment and papyrus.—Palimpsests.

THE toleration of Christianity (A. D. 311), and its subsequent establishment as the religion of the State under Constantine, naturally led to the organization of a greater number of schools, and a larger attendance upon those already established; but the troublous times which followed in the Western Empire, and the constant immigration of the barbaric races into Italy for two centuries, not only operated as a check upon literature and intellectual progress, but greatly debased and modified the Latin language, so that the Latin of the Augustan age was hardly understood by the inhabitants of Italy in the sixth century.

In the Eastern Empire a higher civilization and a more generous culture prevailed, for a time; and Constantinople and the other cities of the East had their schools and literature, and cultivated science and the arts, after ignorance and barbarism had overspread the West.

It will aid us to form some estimate of the education of the fifth and sixth centuries, in the Western Empire, and indeed throughout Europe, if we examine, briefly, the text-books in general use at that period. The course of instruction in the schools was divided into the Trivium, which embraced grammar, logic or dialectics, and rhetoric; and the Quadrivium, which included arithmetic, geometry, astronomy, and music.

The usual, and indeed the almost universal, text-book in all these studies, for nearly a thousand years, was the *Satira* or *Satyricon* of Marcianus Mineus Felix Capella, an encyclopedia, in nine books, of these sciences, in which prose and poetry alternated about equally. This singular work, which has come down to our own times, was written about A. D. 470. The first two books are entitled "*De Nuptiis Philologiæ et Mercurii*," and give, with copious verbiage, a narrative of the adventures of Mercury in search of a spouse, his rejection by *Sophia* (wisdom) and *Psyche* (the soul), and his final wooing of *Philologia;* the subsequent books introduce, in turn, the children of this redoubtable pair, in character, beginning with Grammar, armed with the needful implements of her art, and recounting her history and achievements; she is followed, successively, by Dialectics, Rhetoric, Geometry, Arithmetic, Astronomy, and Music, each of whom declares her attainments, in alternate verse and prose.

The meagerness of the instruction in these studies may be inferred from the fact that the Arithmetic occupies but a brief space, and gives only the digits and their fractions, without any valuable instruction even in the elementary rules. It is mainly occupied with discussions concerning the virtues of certain numbers. The Grammar is equally brief, and dwells principally upon the names and powers of the letters. The Geometry is very little better, though Euclid's work was not rare. The other books, except that on dialectics, are nearly valueless. Aristotle was the basis of all dialectic instruction, though his works were not available in Latin till a few years later.

The only formidable rivals of Capella, in the publication of these encyclopedic text-books, were Cassiodorus and Isidore, who flourished in the sixth century. Their works are even more meager in instruction than that of Capella,—the Arithmetic of Cassiodorus occupying but two folio pages, and not containing a word even of the elementary rules of the science. His Geometry occupies about the same space, and contains only a few axioms. The Grammar and Rhetoric are of about equal value. Music then, as later, was confined mostly to church chanting; and Astronomy was only a brief epitome of the system of Ptolemy, and did not even explain the cause of eclipses. Capella, indeed, like some of his predecessors, seems to have had some dim idea of the possibility that the earth revolved around the sun, but only sufficient to suggest it vaguely. And these books were the text-books for the next thousand years! and even in these, few went beyond the *Trivium.*

One name illumines the fast-gathering darkness of the period—BOETHIUS (*q. v.*), born 455, or, as some say, 470 A. D., and executed, by the order of Theodoric, king of the Ostrogoths, 526. Boethius was the last link which connected the learning and accomplishments of the Augustan age with the darkness of the middle ages. Learned in all the literature of Greece and Rome, a writer worthy of the golden age of Rome, an inventor and discoverer in astronomical and mathematical science, and an ardent friend and patron of education, he had fallen upon evil times. Though for many years a favorite of the illiterate but energetic Theodoric, who at first seemed to take pleasure in furthering his efforts for the diffusion of education, he finally fell under his displeasure, in part from his efforts to instruct the countrymen of the monarch, the Ostrogoths, whose ignorance and contempt of education gratified their king. Boethius translated several of Aristotle's and Plato's works, and himself wrote treatises on arithmetic, rhetoric, music, geometry, and the quadrature of the circle. He also translated the works of Euclid, Archimedes, and Ptolemæus of Alexandria. But his works were too learned for the age in which he lived, and seem never to have come into very general use. The intellectual nadir of the world was approaching; in the seventh century ignorance sounded its lowest depths.

Isidore, bishop of Seville (born 570, died 636), is almost the only man of this period of darkness, who could lay claim to any considerable scholarship, and his attainments in science would be regarded as exceedingly meager in our times; yet he was, at that day, considered a prodigy of learning.* It is recorded, to his

* The fathers of the 8th Council of Toledo, decreed him publicly the most fulsome eulogies, and spoke of him in their capitularies in the

honor, that he attempted to diffuse education among his clergy, and established a school at Seville. He also prepared an encyclopedia, near the close of his life, in which he attempted to give to the world a compendium of the knowledge which appeared so vast to his cotemporaries.

This work, entitled *Origines, seu Etymologiarum libri*, was in twenty books. The first three were devoted to the seven liberal arts (the *trivium* and *quadrivium*), and may be supposed to furnish a *résumé* of his knowledge in regard to them; but they do not contain one-tenth of the information to be found in our most elemetary school-books. Under the head of Arithmetic, for instance, he only explains that arithmetic and the names of numbers were derived from the Greek, speaks of their usefulness, especially in enabling us to understand the mystic sense of some passages

---

following terms: *Doctor egregius, Ecclesiæ Catholicæ novissimum decus, præcedentibus ætate postremus, doctrinæ comparatione non infimus, atque, et quod majus est, jam sæculorum finitorum doctissimus, cum reverentia nommandus, Isidorus.* It is difficult to imagine what more they could have said in the way of eulogy.

of Scripture, and divides them into even and odd numbers; and then proceeds to speak of geometry. In grammar, he has evidently no knowledge of syntax and very little of etymology; he confounds rhetoric with dialectics, and considers astrology a valuable department of astronomical knowledge. The remaining books of the *Origines* are occupied with such topics as these: Medicine, Law, the Scriptures, God, an account of heretics and their opinions, Languages, of which he specifies three principal ones—Hebrew, Greek, and Latin; a Latin dictionary, with very fanciful derivations; Man, and the parts of the body; Animals; the World, and its visible phenomena; Geography, Great Cities, Precious Stones, Agriculture; War, the Drama, &c.; miscellaneous subjects, and Food.

On most of these topics the ideas enunciated are crude, fanciful, often indeed absurd. Yet, if we compare the attainments necessary for the preparation of such a work with those possessed by the kings, nobles, and even the bishops and inferior clergy of his time, we can readily understand why he should have had so exalted a reputation for learning.

Of the kings then reigning in Europe, very few were able to read, and still fewer to write; their courtiers were, of course, equally ignorant; ability to read and write was not considered, by any means, indispensable even to the bishops, much less to the inferior clergy. The monasteries generally contained libraries, and some of the monks could usually write well enough to transcribe such copies of the Scriptures or liturgy as were needed; but this was done in so imperfect and slovenly a manner that their manuscripts were full of errors, and a century or two later required the most strenuous efforts for their correction.

Schools were attached to the cathedrals and the monasteries, and had been, in many cases, since the latter part of the fourth century; but the children were, at this period, seldom taught either to read or write. The ability to repeat and chant the *Credo*, the *Pater-noster*, the *Ave Maria*, and a few Latin hymns, without any idea of their signification, was the extent of their instruction. The importation of papyrus from Egypt had ceased; cotton and linen paper were yet unknown in Europe, and parchment was costly and difficult of preparation. The great libraries of Alexandria, of Rome, and of Constantinople had perished by fire; and the illiterate monks knew just enough to efface the writing from the few valuable parchments in their libraries, and cover them anew with silly legends, the product of brains muddled with intoxicating liquors. The chemical skill of modern times has enabled us to discharge the ink from many of these *palimpsests*, and restore the classical works so ruthlessly destroyed.

CHAPTER XI.

Education in the British Isles.—CHARLEMAGNE, the most efficient friend of education at this period.—His invitation to Alcuin.—His Capitularies.—Services of Alcuin in promoting education.—Paul the Deacon, Peter of Pisa, Clement the Hibernian, and Raban Maur also rendered valuable service.—Alfred the Great, the educational reformer of Britain.—Saracen learning at this period.—Eminent Jewish scholars of the time.

THE British isles were not, at this period, reduced to quite so low a condition of ignorance as the continental countries. Education was not, indeed, diffused generally among the people, but the cloistral schools at York, Canterbury, Oxford, Cambridge, Dublin, and perhaps some other points, were decidedly in advance of any of those on the continent. St. Patrick, Colomba, Willebrod, Aelbert, John of Beverley, bishop of Hagulstad,—a man of learning for his times, and so zealously disposed in favor of education that he even attempted the instruction of a deaf mute,—Ceolfric, abbot of the cloistral school at

Wearmouth, and the Venerable Bede, the early ecclesiastical historian of England,—all flourished in this and the preceding century, as did also St. Boniface, also a native of England, whose labors and martyrdom, in the attempt to promote the education, civilization, and Christianization of the rude Frisians, are deserving of commemoration.

The first movement, however, looking toward any material progress in education, occurred during the reign of the Emperor Charlemagne (A. D. 768–814). Though himself, in the early part of his career, illiterate and unable to write, this energetic prince possessed wisdom enough to appreciate the advantages of education to his people, and its necessity for those who administered either civil or ecclesiastical power. In his tour through Italy, about A. D. 780, he met with several men of considerable learning, and was so much impressed with the importance of intellectual improvement that he urged the most eminent of them, Alcuin, an Anglo-Saxon, born in Brittany, but educated at

York, England, and at that time at the head of a cloistral school established by the archbishop of York, to come to his court and take up his residence there.

Alcuin at first declined, but, after repeated solicitation, acceded to his request, and, in 782, became a member of the emperor's household. So eager was Charlemagne for learning, that he placed himself and all the members of his family under the instruction of Alcuin, who taught the trivium and quadrivium to the princes, nobles, and courtiers of the realm; thus establishing, or at least reviving, in an improved form, the *aulic* or *palatine* school of the Merovingian kings. Alcuin was probably the most learned man of his time; but though his attainments at a later period would not have been deemed remarkable, he is deserving of honor for the efforts to which he prompted his imperial pupil for the promotion of education throughout his empire. Through his influence the cathedral schools were reopened, and their course of study enlarged and elevated; the manuscripts of the old Roman literature brought to light, corrected, and for the first time punctuated, and, to some extent, restored as text-books in the schools, from which they had been banished on theological grounds.

In two *Capitularies*, issued 787 and 788, addressed by Charlemagne to the religious preachers under his government, and to Bangulf, a celebrated abbé, the head of a religious order, and his congregations, the emperor insists on a higher education for the priesthood, the multiplication of correct copies of the Scriptures and of the Latin classics, and the teaching of these and of the liberal arts, by the priests and monks, to the pupils of the schools. In the administration of his school of the palace and his other educational enterprises, Charlemagne was also aided by Paul the Lombard Deacon, Clement the Hibernian, and Peter of Pisa, all of them men eminent, in that dark period, for learning and intellectual ability.

Alcuin withdrew from the court, on account of age and infirmity, in 796, but established an excellent school at his abbey of St. Martin of Tours, where he died in 804. Several of his pupils also became distinguished as teachers, the most eminent of whom, Raban Maur, succeeded him in the Palatine school; and had the clergy seconded the efforts of Alcuin and Charlemagne for the general promotion of education, the intellectual dawn need not have been postponed for seven centuries; but exertion and study were not suited to their dispositions, and on the death of Charlemagne there was a gradual relapse, which, despite the efforts of Louis le Debonnaire and Charles the Bald, well-nigh obliterated the progress which had been made during his administration.

This much, however, had been gained: the cathedral and conventual schools, which, if not broken up by the civil wars which preceded his reign, had, at least, been rendered nearly worthless, were restored, and the character of their teachings elevated; the German language had been recognized as a medium for instruction, and the Scriptures, as well as some text-books, translated into it; and there were scattered through the vast domains of the emperor a few learned men (learned *i. e* for the time), who would seek the promotion of science and the improvement of education.

The next remarkable patron of education was Alfred the Great, of England (A. D. 849–900). The civil disorders which preceded his reign and which occupied the earlier portions of it, the repeated and destructive invasions of the Danes, and the consequent misery and poverty of the people, the destruction of the convents and cloistral schools and the valuable libraries which they contained, had plunged the inhabitants of England into a depth of ignorance and wretchedness of which they had no previous experience.

It was under circumstances thus discouraging, and while himself involved in almost interminable wars, that Alfred turned his attention to the intellectual improvement of his people. With the exception of a portion of Bishop Isidore's works and the gospel of St. John, which had previously been translated into Anglo-Saxon by the Venerable Bede, there seem to have been no books in the vulgar tongue; and Alfred, rightly judging that the cultivation of the spoken language of a people was one of the first steps toward their mental culture, translated with his own hands, amid his other cares, the works of Bede, Orosius, and the *Consolations of Philosophy* of Boethius, and induced others to undertake the translation of other works. To teach the young to read these books, and also some of those in the Latin, was his next effort; and, under his fostering care, the monastic schools were revived, endowments were bestowed upon them, and the strongest inducements he could offer were set before the most eminent scholars of the time to take charge of them.

Among those who accepted his invitation, and aided according to their ability, were Grimbald, a French monk, John, surnamed the Saxon, St. Neoth, Asser, subsequently his biographer, Plegmond, archbishop of Canterbury, Dunwulf, afterwards bishop of Worcester, Gerbert, bishop of Chester, Wulfsig, and Athelstan, bishop of London; and, most renowned of them all, John Scotus, called Erigena, to whom some writers attribute the origin of the scholastic philosophy. Oxford was, during Alfred's reign, and had been, indeed, for two or three centuries, renowned for its schools, connected, for the most part, with the monasteries.

Under the genial influence which Alfred exerted in behalf of education, these schools were a popular resort for scholars; and hence some writers have attributed to him, but without any just authority, the establishment of the University of Oxford,—an event which, so far as its formal or public recognition was concerned, did not take place till nearly three centuries later.

In England, however, as in France, the impulse given to education by its liberal and enlightened monarch, did not long survive his death, and the tenth century is usually reckoned, by English writers, the darkest period of its history. It can hardly be said, however, that the darkness was as profound over the whole of Europe as in the seventh century.

We have already spoken of the Saracen conquests in Sicily and Spain, and of their cultivation of science and literature at a period when ignorance had overspread the rest of Europe. In the tenth century they were approaching that intellectual eminence, which, in the two succeeding centuries, they so fully maintained; and here and there a Christian scholar, athirst for knowledge, ventured to Cordova, Granada, or Seville, and quaffed it from Moslem fountains.

Their influence, too, was felt in other countries. Through their Sicilian colony they introduced paper, made from cotton and linen rags, into Europe; and if they were not the inventors of what are usually known as the Arabic numerals,—recent discoveries making it probable that all, except the cipher, were known to Boethius,—they certainly first came into general use from their teachings; algebra, too, seems first to have been taught in their schools, and the scholars of Christendom began to discover that mathematical studies were of some use for other purposes than to interpret the mystical sense of the numbers used in the Scriptures. Chemical science was also introduced by them; and though we cannot but regret the years and intellect wasted in the researches of alchemy, we may be comforted by remembering the numerous discoveries which were incident to it. Medical science, too, was confined, for several centuries, to the Saracens and the Jews, who made commendable progress in it.

The Jews, indeed, were more eminent, in general scholarship, than any of the nations among whom they dwelt, and, but for the social disabilities under which they labored, might have exerted a favorable influence upon the intellectual condition of Christendom. Sedecias, the physician of Charles the Bald, David Mosel, Aben Zoar, Benjamin of Tudela, Solomon ben Jarchi, Judah Cohen, and Savasorda are a few of the eminent men of this persecuted race, who, in the schools of France, Italy, and Spain, did much service in the cause of education.

CHAPTER XII.

Universities in Italy in the eleventh and twelfth centuries.—Departments of law and medicine established.—Schools of the Benedictine and other monastic orders.—Cause of the establishment of universities.—The scholastic philosophy and its founders.—Its influence.—Condition of education in the Eastern Empire.—The efforts of the dynasty of Comnenus for its improvement.—Downfall of the Eastern Empire.—Reflex influence upon Russia.

In Italy, the gradual improvement in intelligence and learning began early in the twelfth century to exhibit itself in the organization of universities, of which those of Bologna and Salerno were the earliest examples. Both originated, as did most of the earliest European universities, in schools which, under a succession of able teachers, had acquired renown in some particular branch of instruction. Bologna had maintained such a school, in high repute for legal science, from the early part of the eleventh century, and perhaps even earlier; and in the beginning of the twelfth century, its professors were often called upon to solve knotty legal questions, by the rulers of the adjacent States.

In 1137, Wernerius, one of the most eminent jurists of the middle ages, published and expounded to a vast concourse of students his *Pandects.* Other sciences were also taught there, and the University of Bologna seems to have existed in fact, though not in name, from the early part of the twelfth century. It was incorporated in 1228. Salerno had, about the same period, acquired a similar reputation in medicine.

In this review of the few lights whose glimmering only rendered the darkness more visible, we must not forget the services rendered to education by some of the monastic orders. Though too many of these led lives of mere sensual indulgence, and gloried in their ignorance, some were inspired with a nobler ambition, and sought to render the monastic life of benefit to the world, as its founders had intended.

The monks of the Benedictine order had, from their foundation, devoted themselves to the work of teaching; and, under the wise and energetic management of Odon, abbé of Cluny (927 A. D.), they regained much of their early efficiency. The new orders of Chartres and Citeaux, founded about the close of the eleventh century, were also of material service in maintaining the monastic schools. Germany was most benefited by these labors. The conventual schools of Fulda, Corbie, Hildesheim, Paderborn, Hersfeld, and Hirschau, became renowned in the tenth and eleventh centuries, not less for the eminent men who presided over them than for the extension of the instruction beyond the *seven liberal arts*. Painting and poetry, and the Greek and Latin literature of the classic ages, were taught, and libraries, with very considerable collections of books, were founded.

The cathedral and collegiate schools even surpassed the conventual, in their curriculum of study and in their freedom in the use of the Latin and Greek authors. But this freedom was confined to Germany. Elsewhere throughout Christendom the Greek and the Latin of the Augustan age were prohibited studies, and fierce anathemas were hurled at those who sought to acquire them. Even the bishops most zealous in the cause of education were fain to content themselves with requiring that the inferior clergy should be able to understand the liturgy, or, if this was too much, that they should at least be able to pronounce it correctly and recite it without omissions. The clergy being thus illiterate, the laity, as might be expected, were still more so. A layman who knew how to write was reckoned almost a prodigy; in many of the schools writing was not taught, and paper was yet so scarce that, when taught, black surfaces, like our blackboards, were used for writing, or the pupils were required to furnish wax tablets. In 1291, the Abbé and the entire Chapter of St. Gall did not know how to write.

The organization of a number of universities during the twelfth and thirteenth centuries, and the new impulse thus given to learning, did something to prevent the darkness of ignorance from entirely enshrouding the nations. Twenty-three universities, including those of Paris, Oxford, Cambridge, Montpellier, Toulouse, Bologna, Salerno, Padua, Naples, Salamanca, Rome, and Lisbon, date from these two centuries.

We should deceive ourselves, however, were we to attribute this sudden establishment of so many institutions of learning to a revival of letters, or a thirst for really scientific attainments. It was the era of the schoolmen; the scholastic philosophy, whose essence lay in nice distinctions, in subtle quibbles, and in the artful fence of dialectics,—a philosophy which some writers imagine was first taught by John Scotus, called Erigena, in the ninth century, but which had attracted but little attention till the eloquence and logical ability of Roscellinus, of William of Champeaux, and the renowned Abelard, at the close of the eleventh and the beginning of the twelfth century, drew listening thousands to their discussions and prelections,—now fascinated the intellect of Christendom; and though, at the present day, the questions they discussed and the distinctions they drew seem trivial, puerile, and foolish, yet, for two centuries and more, they so agitated the minds of pope and prelate, of cowled monk and priestly father, of cleric and laic, of doctors of law and of theology, that the universities which had been created as battle-grounds for these doughty champions of a wordy war, were crowded with students from all parts of Christendom.

These dialectic conflicts, wearisome as they now are to the reader, accomplished much in developing freedom of thought, and in preparing the way for further progress in education. The biographers of Luther attribute his power as a debater, and his skill as a reasoner, to his thorough mastery of the works of the schoolmen, and especially to his familiarity with the *Summa Theologia* of Thomas Aquinas.

But while thus tracing the educational progress of western Europe, we must not wholly overlook the condition of the Eastern Empire, which, at this period, was tottering to its fall. From the sixth century, there had been a gradual decay of all institutions for the promotion of learning, up to the period of the dynasty of Comnenus; and if, at times, the voluptuous and effeminate monarchs, ruled by women and eunuchs, established some schools at Constantinople, their influence was not felt beyond the circle of the court. Philosophy was indeed taught in their schools, but it was the half-comprehended philosophy of Aristotle and Plato, with the stupid glosses of the Neo-platonists.

With the accession of Isaac Comnenus to the throne, 1057 A. D., there were symptoms of a deeper interest, on the part of the emperor, for the intellectual improvement of his people. The schools of Constantinople acquired a high reputation. The ancient classics were introduced into them, and into the conventual schools of the empire; and though theology formed too large a share of the instruction, still there were more indications for good than in any previous period of its history. His successors of that dynasty followed in his footsteps, and, though possessing no great energy of character, promoted learning to the extent of their ability.

Toward the end of the twelfth century, Constantinople was exposed to repeated pillage; and the French emperors who, in the thirteenth century, established the Latin Empire there, had no sympathy with the people whom they had conquered, and no desire for their intellectual culture. Trebisond, indeed, and some other of the small independent principalities, maintained schools within their own boundaries; but, over the empire in general, darkness reigned. The accession of Michael Palæologus marks another, but futile, effort to restore and improve the schools of his domain; but centuries of misrule had done their work on the empire, and its subsequent history is one of constant and rapid deterioration, till at last it fell a prey to the Osmanlis.

Russia first appears on the stage, as a Christian power, in the latter part of the tenth century, and its subsequent connection with the Eastern Roman Empire, especially in matters of education, was intimate. From Constantinople came its teachers and its bishops, and its intellectual culture varied with that of the Roman capital. In the latter years of the decline of Constantinople, many of its choicest books were removed to Moscow, and the great library of the Patriarchs was founded in that city; but Russian education did not, during the middle ages, rise above its source, and, so far as the masses of the people were concerned, came far short of it.

CHAPTER XIII.

Scholasticism and mysticism in Western Europe.—Course of study in the universities in the thirteenth and fourteenth centuries.—Colleges.—Establishment of gymnasia and trivial schools in Germany. —Bacchantes and A. B. C. shooters.—Hardships of the latter.—The introduction of linen and cotton paper.—Text-books of the period. —Severity of the school discipline.—Eminent friends of education among the mystics.—Female education much neglected during this period.

We return to Western Europe, where, in spite of the darkness, there was more of intellectual life than in the effete Oriental Empire. The events of the twelfth, thirteenth, and fourteenth centuries, which had most influence on education, were the formal organization of university instruction, the prevalence of the scholastic philosophy, and its rival and enemy, *mysticism*, and the changes effected by the Crusades.

We have already spoken of the origin of most of the universities in schools of greater or less repute, in which the *trivium* and *quadrivium* were taught, and, in some instances, one or more branches of professional education also; it was not until the thirteenth century that these schools were formally recognized and endowed with money, and with those numerous and peculiar privileges which made them often formidable in the civil and ecclesiastical conflicts of a later period; and at first, except in the University of Paris, where theology was taught, that of Salerno, which was the seat of medical learning, and that of Bologna, where the science of law was prosecuted, they seem not to have gone beyond the *seven liberal arts* in their instruction.

Soon, however, the course of study was expanded; and, in addition to professional education which was given in the greater part (faculties of theology, law, and medicine being organized), the popes, for the most part reluctantly, and with many cautions and prohibitions,* licensed additional professors.

* From the number of the popes who were opposed to education, justice requires that we should except Gerbert, who was elected to the pontifical chair in 999, under the title of Sylvester II. Gerbert was one of the most eminent scholars, as well as one of the most liberal and catholic spirits, of his time. After acquiring what of science could

Thus we find that, in 1312, professorships of Hebrew, Arabic, and Chaldee were established by the pope, at Rome, Paris, Oxford, Bologna, and Salamanca. These languages were doubtless regarded as less harmful than the classic Latin; for Fritz tells us that, in 1228, Gregory IX. prohibited all instruction in the Latin classics, and that, in 1254, not only had *belles-lettres* ceased to be cultivated, even in the University of Paris, but the names of Cicero and Virgil were unknown to the students, and the rules of prosody utterly ignored. Toward the end of the fourteenth century, the University of Vienna, then recently established (founded A. D. 1365), gave instruction in physics and mathematics.

The colleges—originally only halls, endowed by benevolent individuals to furnish lodging, and in some instances food also, to the students, but which soon came to have their

---

be learned in the best schools of Christendom, he had crossed the Pyrenees, and, in the Saracen university of Toledo, had mastered the learning of the Arabian scholars. Unfortunately, his career as pope was too brief (he died in 1003) to permit him to accomplish much for the cause of education, which he had so much at heart.

masters, tutors, and special regulations, restraining those who were on their foundations from the riotous and licentious lives of those who were students at large—also exerted some influence in promoting a higher scholarship.

In Germany a series of schools were created, preparatory for the universities, and known under the various names of *trivial*, from the pupils studying only the *trivium; gymnasia*, in which philosophy and history were also taught, and *academic gymnasia*, which, though pursuing a course of study as extensive as the universities, had not the power of conferring degrees. In the fourteenth century, a practice prevailed almost universally, over Middle and Southern Europe, which resulted in part, doubtless, from the adventurous spirit introduced by the Crusades.

At first, the masters, teachers, and professors of the schools and universities wandered from one university town to another, seeking perhaps new ideas, though oftener, doubtless, prompted by the desire of a higher compensation; soon the students began also to lead a vagrant life, and, under the name of Bacchantes, roamed over the different university towns of Europe, studying a little, but for the most part leading a riotous and lawless life, and often spending many years in their travels. Possessing many immunities and privileges as students, they took many more, and became, at last, the terror of the towns they visited.

It was their practice to attach to themselves very considerable numbers of young boys, whom they professed to teach the elements of reading and grammar, but whom they really employed to forage for them, requiring them, by begging or stealing, to procure their food, and beating them cruelly if they failed to do so. Of the hardships endured by these children, who were called *A. B. C. shooters*, Platter, a Swiss scholar of the sixteenth century, who had been one of them, gives a most interesting account in his autobiography.

The Crusades had impoverished many of the countries of Europe, and had thus, perhaps, proved unfavorable to the cause of education; but they had awakened the intellect of the people from its deathlike slumber, had enlightened their minds as to the productions and learning of other countries, had evoked a spirit of enterprise, and promoted commerce, which, for its efficient operation, required a certain amount of education, greater than that as yet possessed by the people generally.

The manufacture of paper in Venice, which followed the introduction of it into Italy during the Crusades, also exerted a powerful influence in the promotion of education, by multiplying books. The text-books of this period, however, contained little of value in the way of instruction; the *Satyricon* of Capella, the *Grammar* of Donatus, and the *Doctrinal*, a grammatical treatise composed by a Franciscan monk of Brittany, and inferior in merit even to Donatus, were the only ordinary text-books; to go beyond these required a special permission from the ecclesiastical authorities; and the schools and pupils thus favored, were taught the symbols of the apostles, the penitential psalms, the canticles of the Church, the *Morals* of Cato, the *Eclogues* of Theodulus (a very brief sacred history), the *Regulæ Pueriles*, the *Consolations of Philosophy* of Boethius, and a few other works, of similar character, but less merit. Geography, history, the mathematics, and the physical sciences were utterly neglected.

But if the teachers bestowed but little instruction, they enforced that little by a very severe discipline. The title-page of almost every text-book of this period, is adorned with a picture of the master armed with a bunch of rods. The code of the school at Worms, in 1260, provided "that any pupil whose bones have been broken, or who has been severely wounded by his master, in chastising him, shall have the right of quitting the school without paying the *honorarium.*"

We have already spoken of the rise and influence of the scholastic philosophy. Its quibbles and puerilities disgusted some of the most earnest and devoted men of the Romish Church, and the mystical philosophy was the result of their protest against it. Among the most eminent advocates of this philosophy, were Bernard of Clairvaux, Thomas a Kempis, John Tauler, and Jean Charlier de Gerson, who, though at first, from his position as chancellor of the University of Paris, disposed to the views of the schoolmen, later in life sympathized fully with the mystics. Several of these men were eminent for scholarship, and were successful teachers. Gerson wrote a work on the moral and religious education of children, which is still preserved. It is of little value, except as showing what were the views of enlightened men of that age on the subject of education. Vincent de Beauvais and Hugues de St. Victor, in the twelfth century, also wrote brief treatises on pedagogy. That of the latter, on the method of instruction, though too essentially theological, is a work of considerable merit.

During this period (from the eleventh to the fourteenth century), female education was at a low ebb; a few schools for the instruction of girls in reading were maintained in the larger cities, but beyond this they received very little mental culture. In the convents, they were taught to repeat their prayers, to practice embroidery and other needle-work, and, too often, to indulge in intrigues with the monks. A distinguished writer of the thirteenth century defines the proper education of woman, as "knowing how to pray to God, to love man, to knit and to sew." From the time when the gifted but ill-fated Heloise, in the twelfth century, taught to her nuns the Greek and Latin classics and the sciences then known, to the latter part of the fifteenth century, Western Europe furnishes no female name renowned for learning, except that of Christina of Pisa (1363–1431). In the Eastern Empire, the names of the Empress Eudocia and Anna Comnena show that, in the court circles at least, the culture of the intellect was not deemed inappropriate to woman.

CHAPTER XIV.

Chivalry, and its influence upon education.—The celebration of the deeds of its heroes in song.—Troubadours, Trouveres, and Minnesingers.—*Chansons* and *sirventes*.—Revival of literature in Italy in the fourteenth century.—Formative influence on the languages of Europe.—Emigration of Chrysoloras and other eminent Greek teachers to Southern Europe.—Prevalence of the study of classic Greek.—Vittorino da Feltre, one of the most eminent teachers of the age.—The patronage of letters by the Medici and other Italian sovereigns.—Eminent scholars and teachers in Italy.—Gerard Groot and the Brethren of the Common Life.—Establishment of the schools of Eton and Winchester in England.

THERE remains to be noticed still one more source of educational influence affecting this period, before we speak of the revival of letters, which commenced in the fourteenth century—viz.: chivalry, and the literature of the Troubadours, Trouveres, Minnesingers, and bards, which grew naturally out of it. The highest development of chivalry was the result of the Crusades; it had existed before the first of them, and was probably an institution of Moorish origin; but in the sacrifices, the toils, sufferings, bravery, and heroism of the knights of the Crusades, it reached its culmination.

The education of the knight was rather physical and moral than intellectual. Many of the most noble and distinguished knights could not read; still more of their number could not write; but all, at least in the early days of chivalry, had so cultivated their physical powers, as to be able to endure hardships, to undergo long and fierce contests, to make light of wounds, and to be agile, and skillful in the use of weapons and the management of their steeds. They had also learned to be courteous to the weak, to entertain a Platonic affection for some one or more of the fair sex, whose honor, purity, and beauty they maintained against all comers, to succor the feeble and distressed, and to regard, with the highest reverence, the virtues of truth, honor, and chastity.

It was natural that the virtues and noble deeds of such men should be embalmed in song; and, in that age, it was considered to argue no lack of modesty on the part of the hero, if he recounted, in the soft Provençal tongue, or in the Italian language, equally fitted for song, the deeds of daring he had attempted, and the victories he had won.

Those who wooed the fair, whose colors they had worn, with their sonnets, in which amatory verse mingled with the narration of their deeds, were, in the Langue d'Oc or Provençal language, called *Troubadours;* in the Langue d'Oil, *Trouveres;* and among the Germans, *Minnesingers* (Minnesanger). After a time these songs were divided into two classes —the *chansons*, or amatory songs, and the *sirventes*, or songs of a warlike, and sometimes of a satiric, or even didactic character. The character of this poetry is not very high, probably owing to the fact that its authors were mostly illiterate; but among the troubadours were found the most powerful monarchs and the most intellectual men of the eleventh and twelfth centuries, Frederic Barbarossa, Richard Cœur de Lion, several of the kings of France, the Comte de Provence, and many others of similar rank, being among the number; and not a few of their productions are devoted to the subject of the education of knights, cavaliers, and high-born dames.

The overwhelming corruption which followed the Crusades, however, soon dragged down, to its own level, the lofty principles of chivalry; the platonic love of its earlier days subsided into a grosser passion, its honor dwindled into mere courtesy, and its brave defence of the weak and the distressed into the raids and conflicts of civil war. The lessons of obedience, truth, honor, and fidelity, which the chevalier had learned in his various service of page, esquire, and knight, were no more taught, and chivalry at last grew to be a subject for the ridicule of brilliant wits. Long ere this its literature had degenerated, and the *chansons* and *sirventes* of the earlier times were replaced by odes and songs too gross to be tolerated.

The fourteenth century was remarkable as the period when the languages of Europe attained a more perfect development, and became fixed in substantially their present forms. The Italian, now universally acknowledged the best adapted of them all for poetry, improvisation, and song, first showed its wonderful flexibility in the writings of Dante Alighieri, Petrarch, and Boccacio, during that century; the Spanish did not develop its full powers till a century later; the French was, under the fostering care of the University of Paris, rapidly improving as an admirable medium for earnest debate and animated conversation; the German, with its Suabian element largely increased by the popular songs of the Minnesingers, was taking form and shape to become, a hundred and fifty years later, the vehicle of the vigorous eloquence of the Reformers; while the English was almost created, in its written form, by the genius of Chaucer. Hitherto, these languages could hardly be said to have had any grammatical principles; the attempt to bend them to the old Latin rules had introduced so many anomalies, that the task of adhering to grammatical constructions was beyond the ability of most writers; but, after the advent of the writers we have named, new views prevailed, and the languages were thenceforth subordinated only to rules drawn from the most natural construction of each.

The tottering condition of the Eastern Empire caused the more eminent of its scholars (and the last century of its existence was notable for quite a number of these) to migrate to Italy, and there expand the knowledge of its language and literature. Prominent among them, as successful teachers, were the brothers John and Emmanuel Chrysoloras, who came to Florence in 1397, and there taught the Greek classics and the Platonic philosophy.

At that period, very few of the best scholars of Western Europe were familiar with the Greek, and fewer still knew any thing of Plato. But the constant immigration of learned Greeks into Italy and France, awakened enthusiasm in the study of both the language and the philosophy, and led to the collection and transcription of many Greek and Latin manuscripts, which, up to that period, had remained unknown in the cells and dungeons of the monasteries; yet, for nearly half a century later, Greek was taught in the universities only by emigrants from Greece,—Gregory of Tiferno, in 1458, being the first teacher of Greek, in the University of Paris, who was not himself a Greek.

Among the most eminent teachers of the period of which we are treating, for his attainments in science, his intelligent views in regard to instruction, and his practical tact as a teacher, was Vittorino Rambaldini da Feltre, born 1378, who taught in the University of Padua, and subsequently at Venice and Mantua. It has seldom been the lot of a teacher, who himself wrote nothing on the subject of education, to be so honored by after ages for his success in teaching. Several of the Italian writers give us copious accounts of his system of education. He deemed it the duty of the teacher to exercise a constant supervision over his pupils, and hence he lived with them, and ate at the same table, which was spread with wholesome but plain food. He organized a system of gymnastic exercises, and enforced their regular practice. He taught the rudiments of science very thoroughly, and to his older pupils gave instruction in rhetoric, mathematics, and ethics.

In a corrupt age, he was exceedingly strict in regard to the morals of those under his charge, and appealed in all cases to their own moral sense of the quality of their actions. He studied carefully the temper, disposition, and abilities of each, that he might be able to direct them in their studies and in the selection of a professional course. In his government he was mild but firm, and won the love and friendship of his pupils. Among the distinguished teachers and writers on education, of the fifteenth century, in Italy, were Peter Paul Verger (died 1428), Valla, the most accomplished Latin scholar of his time; Poggio Bracciolini, also an eminent Latinist; Mapheus Vegino (died 1458), and Eneas Sylvius, afterward Pope Pius II.

All of these wrote extensively on educational subjects, and Valla and Eneas Sylvius prepared valuable text-books,—the former in Latin grammar and the Latin classics; the latter in grammar, rhetoric, and universal history. Purbach, Regiomontanus, and Nicolas Cusanus were the first to promote the study of the higher mathematics, and to prepare logarithmic tables. Several of the Italian sovereigns, during this century, were eminent patrons of literature and science; especially the Pope Nicolas V., the founder of the Vatican library; Frederic of Aragon, king of Naples; and, above all, the Medici family, and particularly Cosmo, and Lorenzo the Magnificent. It was owing mainly to their exertions and those of the other sovereigns of Italian States, prompted by rivalry, that Italy, during the fifteenth century, maintained the pre-eminence in arts, science, and literature.

Among the most eminent men of learning, whom this wise and noble policy drew to the Italian cities, were Politian, the author of the *Miscellanea*, and professor of Greek and Latin eloquence at Florence in 1483; Christopher Landino, Hermolaus Barbarus, and, pre-eminent over them all in genius and intellectual power, Lionardo da Vinci. In Spain, toward the close of the century, Lebrexa Nebrissensis, by his own extensive classical learning, and his lectures at Seville, Salamanca, Alcala, and other Spanish universities, effected a reform in classical studies. He also prepared valuable grammars in the Castilian, Latin, Greek, and Hebrew languages.

In Holland, the prevalence of ignorance and vice led one of the noblest men in the Romish Church in that country, Gerard de Groot (1340–1384), to organize the order of *Brethren of the Common Life*, an association resembling, more nearly perhaps than any other, that of the Brethren of the Inner Mission, founded, during the present century, by Dr. J. H. Wichern. This order had little in common with the mendicant friars; its members usually took no vows, provided for their few and simple wants by their daily labor, and devoted themselves to the work of teaching and reforming the ignorant and vicious. The times were favorable to such an organization, and, in a few years, they had more than a hundred congregations, and in less than a century their schools were to be found in most of the larger cities of Germany, Switzerland, Denmark, and the Low Countries. They were opposed by the mendicant friars, but sustained by the popes. Deventer, in Holland, was their principal seat, and from thence, after the death of Gerard, Florence de Radewin, his associate and successor, continued to direct them until his death. In England, the establishment of the great schools of Winchester and Eton, as well as of Winchester College and several others at Oxford, belong to the latter part of the fifteenth century.

CHAPTER XV.

Moral condition of Europe at the close of the fourteenth century and the commencement of the fifteenth.—Invention of the art of printing.—Discovery of America.—Influence of these events in promoting education.—Eminent scholars and teachers in Germany in the fifteenth century.—The dawn of the Reformation in the sixteenth century.—Erasmus, Luther, Melancthon, Zuinglius, and Calvin as educators.—Abundance of Luther's labors for the general diffusion of education.

WHILE, in several of the countries of Europe, considerable intellectual progress had been made, the fourteenth century was, in morals, the darkest of the dark ages. The restraining influence of chivalry was gone, as that of religion had long been; the poverty, lawlessness, and evil manners which had resulted from the Crusades, had fully wrought their direful results; the Roman pontiffs, the cardinals, bishops, and inferior clergy, and, above all, the monastic orders, set examples, which the laity were not slow to follow, of participation in murder, violence, and lust; indulgences for the commission of any crime, except heresy, could be purchased for a trifling sum; and over the extensive realms which acknowledged the power of the Papal See, and the hardly less extensive regions which yielded to the spiritual dominion of the Greek Patriarch, vice and corruption reigned in forms so loathsome and vile that it seemed that nothing less than the waters of a second deluge, or the still more effectual purification of an all-consuming fire, could purge the continent of its guilt.

Two events hastened the upheaval for which the nations were looking: the invention of printing, about 1450, and the discovery of America, in 1492. Hitherto, books had been scarce and costly; multiplied, often at the expense of correctness, by the slow process of copying, they were beyond the reach of all but the wealthy few; the peasantry of Europe were rarely or never taught to read, and if they had been, could not have procured books;—but, under the rapid multiplication of books by the new art, they were to become the property and joy of the masses; and as the discovery of America opened new fields of enterprise and new sources of wealth to crowded Europe, men of intelligence, and at least of moderate education, were in demand, to occupy the newly-discovered lands, and lead the way to richer harvests of wealth and fame.

Amid the general dissoluteness of morals, there were a few noble spirits, who struggled to promote in the minds of their pupils, and in the communities in which they dwelt, higher aspirations and nobler aims. Such were Rodolphe Langius of Westphalia, Maurice of Spielberg, who gave the school at Emmerich a high reputation; Louis Dringenberg of Selestat, Dalberg, Conrad Celtès, Bebel, Beatus Rhenanus, Wimpheling, Pirckheimer, and, a little later, Bishop John of Dahlberg, Rodolphe Agricola of Groningen, to whom, and to Pedro Ponce de Leon, a Spanish Benedictine monk, belongs the honor of having first successfully attempted the instruction of deaf mutes; these and others, who formed a scientific alliance which, under the name of the *Association of the Rhine*, accomplished much for education in Germany in the latter part of the fifteenth century. Reuchlin, too, though perhaps not a professed teacher till near the close of his life, yet rendered good service to classical education, and, by his controversy with Pfefferkorn and the inquisitor Hochstraten, gave a powerful impulse to that freedom of thought which was so soon to revolutionize Christendom. In the first half of the sixteenth century, the Reformation had commenced in Germany, under the labors of Luther, Melancthon, Ecolampadius, Justus Jonas, and others; and in Switzerland and France, under Zuinglius and Calvin.

All these men were, for their time, brilliant and accomplished scholars, and most of them had been engaged in teaching in some of the universities of their respective countries. Erasmus, too, though a man of more timid spirit than the Reformers, was eminent as a teacher, and exerted a powerful influence in the promotion of education. Budæus, universally regarded as the most profound Greek scholar of his time in Europe, also accomplished much for education in France, both by his Greek commentaries and his labors as a teacher. It was reserved, however, for Luther and Melancthon to inaugurate a new era in the cause of education.

Hitherto there had been, as we have already said, no education for the masses; but it was a necessary corollary from Luther's religious principles, that the whole people must be taught, that they might read the Scriptures: hitherto, the teaching of the universities, of the gymnasia, and of the trivial schools, had been mainly directed to the cultivation of the memory; the pupil was not required to reason upon, not even to understand, many of the lessons which he was taught; the memory was taxed with the recollection of vast quantities of rubbish, of little service, either when committed or afterward; but Luther insisted on the development of thought and the culture of the reasoning powers; and, though himself versed in all the subtleties of the scholastic philosophy, he did not deem it well suited to cultivate and invigorate the minds of youth, and therefore denounced it with his usual energy and vehemence.

In 1527, he and his friend Melancthon were directed, by the Elector of Saxony, to investigate the condition of the schools of that country, and, if necessary, to reorganize them. This, by their joint labor, was accomplished, and their plan of instruction published, which provided for the education of children of all classes and both sexes, in the elementary studies, and for a more extended course for those who gave promise of intellectual ability. But Luther's views were too comprehensive to be restricted within the limits of the electorate of Saxony.

In 1524, he had published "*an address to the councilmen of all the towns of Germany*, calling upon them to establish and sustain Christian schools;" and still earlier (in 1520), he had published a plan for reforming the universities, with whose methods of study and course of instruction he was greatly dissatisfied. In all his educational writings (and they were numerous), he inculcated strongly the necessity of a more thorough classical culture, and also of extended mathematical study.

The study of Hebrew, which, if ever taught in the German universities, had been discontinued for a long time, was, at his earnest entreaty, commenced and carried to such extent as the imperfect text-books of the time would allow. History, too, was thenceforth introduced into the curriculum of study, and the scholastic philosophy, and the study of the canon and imperial law, were discarded. In all these reforms he was powerfully seconded by Melancthon, and their united influence induced the changes they desired in many of the German universities, though the scholastic philosophy was slow in yielding to a better system.

In addition to these labors in behalf of education, Luther also appealed to the magistrates of the German cities, to establish libraries for the benefit of scholars; and to his efforts is due the foundation of some of the best public libraries of Germany. Melancthon is deserving of as high praise as Luther, for his zeal in the cause of education, and of the added honor of having been the first to instruct his pupils in the art of teaching, causing them to give instruction in his presence, correcting their errors, and inculcating, both by precept and example, the principles of skillful teaching.

Zuinglius accomplished less for the cause of education than some of his brother reformers, not because his zeal was less, or his capacity inferior, but because his position was different, and his early death gave him less opportunity of usefulness. He, however, reformed and elevated the Academy of Zurich to the rank and character of a university, and gave it such impulses in the right direction, that it has ever since maintained a high rank among the educational institutions of Switzerland. A single essay on the instruction of youth is found among his published works.

Calvin, the mightiest intellect among the Reformers, was also a zealous friend of education, urging the instruction of children, and giving not only his powerful influence, but his personal labors, to the establishment of the Academy of Geneva. His plan of government for Geneva also included the organization of schools for the training of children and youth.

CHAPTER XVI.

JOHN STURM, the most eminent teacher in Germany in the sixteenth century.—Trotzendorf and other eminent cotemporaries of Sturm. —Progress of education in England.—The organization of schools and a system of education by the Jesuits.—Principal features of this system.—M. Villers' characterization of it.—Text-books used by the Jesuits.—The good results they did accomplish.—Decline of the best Protestant schools.

THE most eminent name connected with education in Germany, in the sixteenth century, is that of John Sturm (1507–1589). Trained at first in one of the schools of the "Brethren of the Common Life," at Liege, and afterward a student and teacher at the University of Louvain, he removed, in 1529, to Paris, where he taught, with high reputation, for eight years; when he was invited, by the magistrates of Strasburg, to organize and conduct a gymnasium, or academy of high order, in that city. He removed thither in 1537, and, for forty-one years, remained at the head of the school he had organized.

He possessed, perhaps in a greater degre than any man of his time, that combination c an enthusiastic love for teaching with grea executive powers, which made him the adm ration of the many eminent men with whom h was on terms of intimacy and correspondenc His instructions to his teachers, and his exam nation papers for several years, are still i existence; and they give evidence of a mor thorough and systematic study of the classic than had been previously attempted in th middle ages. He divided his school into te classes, each composed of several *decuriæ* o tens, and placed a teacher over each class His course of instruction was steadily pro gressive, from the tenth class up to the first and his examinations severe and critical. In 1578, more than one thousand pupils attende his instruction. His influence in the thorough organization of gymnasia, throughout Ger many, was very great.

Cotemporary with Sturm was Friedland better known by his patronymic of Trotzen dorf, rector of the academy at Goldberg, in

Silesia, whose methods of instruction and government were novel and efficient. He adhered to the Socratic method in teaching, and was, so far as we know, the first teacher who ever committed the government of his pupils to themselves, organizing them into a court, or senate, to decide on the offences committed and the punishment they merited; the members of this senate being the pupils whose behavior, for a month previous, had been most exemplary.

To him, too, belongs the honor of the first inception of that monitorial system which, long afterward, received its full development from Lancaster and others. Beside Trotzendorf, Bugenhagen at Hamburg, Spalatin at Altenburg, Neander at Nordhausen, and Sylburgius and Heyden at Nuremburg, were distinguishing themselves and benefiting their generation by the introduction of more rational methods of teaching, and by the development of a purer classical taste and a more extended course of study.

Under the united labors of these men and

those whom they had trained as teachers, the Latin authors of the Augustan age became the text-books, in the place of works written in barbarous, monkish Latin; and Greek was as thoroughly understood in Germany as it had been, the previous century, in Italy. Indeed Germany, before the close of the sixteenth century, could boast of more eminent scholars than any other country of Europe.

In England, too, the long period of darkness and ignorance was passing away; and under the fostering care of Grocyn, Cheke, Smith, afterward secretary of state to Queen Elizabeth; Sir Thomas Elyot; and Lily, Cox, Udal, and Norvell, eminent teachers of the time; and, a little later, Roger Ascham (the friend and correspondent of Sturm), Cecil, and others, the schools and colleges of England gradually took a higher position. Ascham was one of the most learned men of the age, and, in his little treatise, "*The Scholemaster*," sought to introduce better methods of instruction and discipline than those usually employed at that period.

The extraordinary progress which was made by the Protestant countries in education, and the great numbers of students, from all countries, who sought instruction in their gymnasia and universities, induced the conviction, on the part of the intelligent adherents of the Romish communion, that unless there were a corresponding advance in their schools and universities, there would be a very serious defection, both in numbers and influence, from their ranks. The monastic schools were urged, but without effect, to introduce improvements and occupy a higher position; even the schools of the Brethren of the Common Life, or *Hieronymians*, as they were now called, in the lapse of two centuries had lost much of their early reputation.

It was at this juncture that the Society of Jesus, organized, in 1540, by Ignatius Loyola, to oppose the heresy of the Reformation, first attempted the organization of schools; and this, like all their other enterprises, was crowned with speedy success. The Jesuit, adroit, supple, versatile, and accomplished, was well qualified for the task before him, in which it was of quite as much importance to know what *not* to teach, as on what topics instruction should be imparted.

An eminent Catholic writer, M. Villers, in a work crowned by the Institute of France, says of their instruction: "It was their maxim to cultivate, and push to the highest possible degree of perfection, every kind of knowledge which would not result in any immediate danger for the hierarchical power, and to acquire thereby the esteem and renown of being the most accomplished and capable scholars of the Christian world. This supremacy once attained, it was easy for them either to paralyze those branches of knowledge which would bear fruit dangerous to the papacy, or to trim, direct, and graft them according to their will." Their text-books were all prepared by members of the order, who, with the utmost skill, molded the facts of history, the reasonings of philosophy, and the principles of theology, to suit their purpose.

The result, to their pupils, was a brilliant, but one-sided education, "fitting them," says M. Villers, "for becoming polished writers, scholars, orators, good Roman Catholics, Jesuits, even, if they wished, but not *men*, in the full acceptation of the term; and he who became a *man* under their discipline, became so independently of it, and in spite of it."

From the *Ratio et institutio studiorum Societatis Jesu*, published in 1599, under the sanction of Claudius de Aquaviva, then general of the order, and which, with slight modifications, is still the educational system of the Jesuit schools, we gather that Latin was taught in these schools, both as a written and spoken language, to the entire disuse of the vernacular, for the use of which penalties were inflicted; that the only classic Latin authors used were Cicero and Virgil, and that, for the rest of the Latin instruction, the pupils were taught from the Latin works of Mediæval writers; that Greek was also taught, but only from the works of Chrysostom and the other Christian fathers; that beyond these *humani-*

ties, as they were called, there were no other studies in the preparatory or lower classes, except grammar (Latin and Greek) and rhetoric. In Greek grammar the Jesuit fathers prepared a very good text-book; in Latin, the old Grammars of Donatus and Priscian were used; neither history, geography, mathematics, nor physical science were taught. This course occupied six years.

The higher course consisted of—FIRST, Philosophy, which occupied two or three years, and which was taught from Aristotle,—the Latin version translated from the Arabic of Averroes, which had been translated from the Syriac, and this from the Greek (as yet there was not known to exist any direct version of Aristotle from Greek into Latin, or any of the vernacular tongues of Western Europe). Aristotle was interpreted according to Thomas Aquinas, the great light of the scholastic philosophy. SECOND, Instruction in morals, from the ethics of Aristotle. THIRD, Mathematics, embracing the elements of Euclid and a few of the simpler problems of mathematical geography.

Then followed a course of theology for those who were deemed suitable candidates for it. Here, so far as the Scriptures were concerned, the Vulgate was the guide, to which all else must be made to correspond; even the Hebrew Scriptures must be read only by the Vulgate. In scholastic theology, Aquinas was again the authority, from whom no deviation was allowed. In casuistry, the genius of the order shone out with peculiar brilliancy, and for the professors of this branch its ablest men were selected.

Emulation was the great incentive to progress among the pupils, and the shameful system of *delation*—that is, acting the part of the spy and tale-bearer, for the purpose of gaining promotion—was regarded as praiseworthy; corporeal punishment was seldom inflicted, and only by persons not members of the order, lest the pupils should be prejudiced against their teachers. The examinations and distributions of prizes were conducted publicly, and with great pomp. Such was the system which, in 1600, had in France alone two hundred schools. Faulty as it was in many particulars, it produced good Latin scholars for that age; and some of the pupils of its schools have hardly been surpassed since that time, in their command of a pure and polished Latin style.

With the death of the leading Reformers, the literary as well as theological activity, which had inspired the ranks of the Protestants, seemed gradually to wane. The Jesuits won many of them back to the Catholic faith, and the most celebrated of their schools lost, wholly or in part, their reputation.

CHAPTER XVII.

The *Novum Organon* of Lord Bacon.—The era of the Classicists. —Rabelais, Montaigne.—Peter Ramus and the Aristotelian philosophy.—Progress in the higher mathematics and in physical science. —The improvements in geographical science.—Stephen's *Thesaurus*. —Constantin, Calepin, and Scapula's dictionaries.—WOLFGANG RATICH.—His new plans, and their faults.—JOHN AMOS COMENIUS, deserving of high honor for his labors in the cause of education.—His *Janua Linguarum Reserata*.—His *Orbis Sensualium Pictus*, the first illustrated school-book.—His other educational works.

THE intellect of Europe had now been thoroughly roused, and the bounds of human knowledge were constantly increasing during the latter half of the sixteenth century. It was at this period that Lord Bacon's *Novum Organon*, perhaps the grandest contribution ever made to science, was published; on the continent of Europe the most eminent classical scholars were endeavoring to correct and improve the text of the Roman and Greek classics,—and most renowned among these, were the Scaligers of Leyden, Casaubon of Geneva, Paulus and Aldus Manutius, and

Sigonius of Italy, Muretus of Paris, Osorius of Portugal, and Sanchez and Alvarez of Spain.

In England, Sir Henry Saville, and Camden, the author of the *Brittania*, worthily maintained the English reputation for classical scholarship; and Andrew Melville, the principal of the University of Glasgow, commenced, in 1575, a thorough reform of that university, which, in a few years, drew students thither from all parts of Europe.

The works of Rabelais, and the essays of Michel de Montaigne, exerted a powerful influence in molding the plans of education of the succeeding age; and Peter Ramus assaulted, with great vigor and effect, the Aristotelian philosophy. The principles of the higher mathematics, though partially discovered in the previous century, were first rendered generally available by Tartaglia, Cardan, Vieta, and perhaps also Pelletier and Bombelli, in algebraic science; Commandin, Clavius, and Maurolycus of Messina, in geometry; and Joachim Rhœticus, in trigonometry. The Copernican theory, though far from being generally received, yet numbered among its advocates Rhœticus, Reinold, Rothman, Christian Wursticius, Maestlin, and the English philosophers Wright and Gilbert, as well as the far more illustrious names of Benedetti and Galileo. Meanwhile, the Danish astronomer Tycho-Brahe was astonishing the world by his astronomical discoveries, and the boldness and daring of his theories; and Kepler was beginning those researches which have made his name immortal.

Physical science was more carefully and extensively cultivated; the laws of optics and mechanics were unfolded by Maurolycus, Bap tista Porta, Guido Ubaldi, Peruzzi, Albrecht Durer, and others; those of statics and hydrostatics, by Galileo and Stevinus; while Gilbert described the use of the magnet. In zoology, Conrad Gesner, the most universally learned man of his time, Belon, Rondelet, Aldrovandus, and Salviani were reducing the chaos of earlier writers to order, and adding new genera and species,—the results of the descriptions and collections of the American adventurers; and in botany, Maranta, Turner, Lobel, Clusius, Caesalpin, Gesner, Dodoens, Dalechampe, Barbier, and Gerard were engaged in a similar work. Of these last, Clusius was by far the ablest, and has left his impress upon the science.

In geography, the expeditions to America had given a new impulse to authorship. Maps began to come into more general use, and one hundred and fifty treatises on geography were published in the last half of the century. Ramusio, Ortelius, Botero, and Mercator are all names which have come down to our own time. It was partly, no doubt, owing to the rapid progress of discovery, that greater attention was paid to philology, and that the Oriental tongues, as well as the languages of the tribes that inhabited the new continent, began to be the objects of study.

The seventeenth century, though beginning with extensive and protracted civil wars, which broke up the schools, and reduced the people to poverty, misery, and semi-barbarism, was yet signalized by the overthrow of old methods of instruction,—especially in the matter of memorizing all lessons, without regard to their meaning, a practice which had come down from the monastic schools of the earlier ages.

A great evil in the classical schools of the previous century, had been the lack of good dictionaries and grammars. This lack had been, in a good degree, supplied in the latter part of the sixteenth century, by the *Thesaurus* of Stephens, the new editions of Constantin and Calepin, and the abridgment of Scapula; and the grammars of Ramus, Sylburgius, Caninius, and Michael Neander;—and with these, and other improved text-books, the desire began to manifest itself for improved methods of teaching.

Wolfgang Ratich (1571–1635) was the first to assail the old system and propose new plans of instruction; but, though a man of learning, he was too conceited and willful, and his plans were too revolutionary and impracticable to meet with any considerable success. He was better qualified to pull down than to build up. His extravagant promises contrasted so strongly with his meager results, that even his well-wishers came to regard him as almost a charlatan. He required the teacher to read over the same lessons to the child again and again, explaining and analyzing every sentence with care; while the child must sit still, and listen in silence,—and this, whether the lesson were a translation, or a chapter of some scientific text-book. In the study of Terence, for example, each section was to be read over by the teacher to his pupils nine times, three times in German and six in Latin. In the hands of Kromayer, Helwig, and some of his other followers, who modified his plans, and made them more practical, the system of Ratich attained to a moderate degree of success.

The most eminent educator of the seventeenth century, however, was JOHN AMOS COMENIUS, bishop of Comna, in Moravia (1592–1671). Comenius saw, more clearly than any of his predecessors, what was necessary for the improvement of education; and his books and principles have exerted a powerful influence over the educational progress of Central and Northern Europe, even to the present day. He was the first to understand the importance of applying the inductive system of Lord Bacon to instruction, and also the first to apply pictures to the illustration of school studies.

His first work, *Janua Linguarum Reserata*, was an attempt to teach Latin (and was equally applicable to other languages), by means of sentences and paragraphs, containing instruction in the elements of all the sciences, each sentence containing Latin words in general use, and these words not being repeated, except when used in a different sense. It contained one hundred chapters and one thousand sentences, and thus taught about eight thousand words.

He begins with a prefatory chapter, explaining his object and design; the second chapter treats of the creation of the world; and in the chapters following, history, arts, and sciences are discussed, the ninety-ninth chapter terminating with the end of the world, and the one-hundredth giving his farewell advice to the reader. This was first published in 1631, but was subsequently much enlarged; and, following out his original conceit, he prepared a *Vestibulum*, of fifty chapters and five hundred sentences, for the use of younger scholars, to precede it, and an *Atrium*, of one hundred chapters and one thousand sentences, to follow it.

The *Janua* was translated into twelve European and several Asiatic languages, and enjoyed a high popularity. His *Orbis Sensualium Pictus*, published in 1657, enjoyed a still higher renown. The text was much the same with the *Janua*, being intended as a kind of elementary encyclopedia; but it differed from all previous school-books, in being illustrated with pictures, on copper and wood, of the various topics discussed in it. This book was universally popular. In those portions of Germany where the schools had been broken up by the "Thirty years' war," mothers taught their children from its pages. Corrected and amended by later editors, it continued, for nearly two hundred years, to be a text-book of the German schools.

His *Methodus Novissima* is also a work of great value to teachers. It is needless, perhaps, to say that, at the present day, Comenius' method of teaching languages has been abandoned, and wiser counsels adopted; but his system was a great advance upon that of Ratich, and a still greater upon that of the teachers of the previous century. He does not seem to have been fully appreciated by later English writers, though, during his lifetime, he was repeatedly solicited, by the highest authorities, to make England his home, and to undertake the reformation of her schools.

CHAPTER XVIII.

The Jansenists, and their labors in the cause of education.—Eminent classical scholars of the seventeenth century.—Progress of literature in Europe during the century.—The School of Pietists.—FÉNELON.—His *Adventures of Telemachus*.—SPENER.—The University of Halle.—FRANCKE.—His philanthropic zeal.—The orphan school, and the institutions connected with it.—Want of classic training, a defect in these schools.—Tendency to Phariseeism subsequently developed.

THE efforts of the Jansenists for the promotion of education, during the seventeenth century, deserve to be recorded. Jansenius was himself a successful teacher; but the eminent men whose defence of his *Augustinus* led them to be called by his name, contended, from the shades of Port-Royal, with their formidable enemies, the Jesuits, in the cause of education, with an ability which deserved, though it did not attain, success. Antoine Arnauld, himself almost a prodigy of learning, found time, amid his other multifarious labors, to reorganize, on a plan of greater efficiency, and with a higher moral tone, several schools.

which attained a high reputation; and also, aided by some of his friends and pupils, to prepare several very good school-books. The Port-Royal Grammar, the joint work of himself and Lancelot, was a popular text-book for more than a century. De Sacy, a nephew of Arnauld, was also eminent as a linguist.

Among the Jesuits, Viger and Labbe wrote, in the early part of the century, treatises of considerable merit on Greek grammar. Casaubon of Geneva, who, in 1610, emigrated to England, stood pre-eminent in critical Greek learning. In Latin, Salmasius, a native of France, but, in the latter part of his life, a resident of Leyden, had no superior; and after his death, the palm on the continent seemed to rest with the two Gronovii, father and son, and Grævius, all residents of Holland.

In England, in the latter part of the century, we find the great name of Bentley, whose learning has hardly been surpassed since the century he adorned. Other names of eminent Latin scholars, some of whom did good service also in the cause of education, will readily recur to the reader. Gruter, Heinsius, Grotius, Barthius, Rigault, Scioppius, Vossius, and Charles Boyle were, perhaps, the most distinguished. Few wrote Latin, either in prose or poetry, with greater elegance and force than John Milton.

The series of classics prepared by about forty of the most eminent scholars of France, at the direction of Louis XIV., *in usum Delphini*, possessed sufficient merit to be retained as classical text-books for more than one hundred and fifty years. In general literature, the seventeenth century was remarkable, above any that had proceded it, for the number of its eminent writers.

In England, the great names of Shakspeare and Milton tower above those of any of their predecessors or cotemporaries ; while those who, in any previous period, would have been considered as occupying the first rank, may be numbered by scores: in France, Corneille, Balzac, Voiture, Malherbe, Racine, Molière, Boileau, La Fontaine, Fontenelle, and many others rendered the court of the "*Grand*

Monarque" the home of *belles-lettres;* in Spain, Cervantes, Lopez de Vega, Calderon, the Argensolas, Villegas, and Gongora abundantly vindicated the richness and beauty of the Castilian tongue; in Italy, Salvator Rosa Guidi, Filicaja, Marini, Tassoni, and Bonarelli attained high distinction; and the works of Opitz, in Germany, and Hooft, in Holland, are still read with pleasure. Nor was the period less remarkable for its philosophers.

No one century, since the Christian era, has produced four such men as Lord Bacon, Descartes, Locke, and Spinosa; nor perhaps even the equals of Arnauld, Gassendi, Malebranche, Hobbes of Malmesbury, and Lord Herbert of Cherbury.

Physical science had received a new impulse from the application to it of the inductive method; and jurisprudence, which had made but small progress since the promulgation of the Code Justinian, and the Capitularies of Charlemagne, seemed suddenly transformed into a new science, through the labors of Grotius, Suarez, Puffendorf, Locke, Leibnitz, and

Godefroy. All this progress exerted its influence upon the promotion of education. The universal activity of intellect stimulated to higher attainment, and to better methods of instruction.

In the latter part of the century, several men of France, Germany, and England, became deeply interested in the promotion of education; and, from the general similarity of their views and aims, writers on education have usually classed them together as the *School of Pietists.* In the loftiness of their ideas, the purity of their lives, and the benevolence of their labors, they remain, to this day, unsurpassed. Prominent among them were Fénelon, archbishop of Cambray, in France; Philip J. Spener, and Augustus Hermann Francke, of Germany.

Fénelon (1651–1715), while yet young, wrote a treatise on the education of girls, which remains, to this day, a work of standard value in France. Subsequently appointed tutor of the grandsons of Louis XIV., one of whom was the heir-apparent to the throne, he displayed a skill, seldom equaled, in their training, and wrote for them some valuable works as text-books, the most celebrated of which, his *Adventures of Telemachus*, will always be a classic, for the purity and beauty of its style, and its elevated moral tone. His "*Fables*," and his "*Dialogues of the Dead*," have also enjoyed a high reputation. Aside from these labors, he was persuaded, by Madame de Maintenon, to draw up a system of education for her favorite female school of Saint Cyr.

Spener (1635–1705) founded the University of Halle, and was for a time the tutor of the two sons of the Prince of Birkenfeld,—beyond which he did little directly in the way of teaching; but he was the founder, among Protestants, of the sect of Pietists, and the friend and adviser of Francke, between whom and himself there existed the most cordial sympathy.

Francke (1663–1727) was one of the most remarkable men of modern times, not so much for his talents—which, however, were respect able—as for his simple, earnest faith, and his entire devotion to the moral and religious education of the young. Chosen professor in the new University of Halle, and, at the same time, pastor of one of the poorest suburbs of that city, he soon resigned his professorship, and, though entirely destitute of property, devoted himself to the improvement of the intellectual and spiritual condition of the poor. With a capital of only seven florins, he commenced his school for orphans, in 1694; and though straitened for means, he struggled on, till oftentimes, as he believed, in answer to his prayers, the necessary funds were sent to him.

In 1705, his orphan house had one hundred boys and twenty-five girls under tuition; his seminary for teachers, who received their board free, had seventy-five pupils,—besides which, sixty-four very poor scholars were supported; a school for the children of citizens had eight hundred scholars and sixty-seven teachers; a *Pædagogium*, or school for the children of the nobility, had seventy pupils; the Oriental College, intended for the training of missionaries to India, eleven pupils; a widows' house, four widows; and a book-store, printing-office, and apothecary's shop employed in all twenty-two persons. Twenty-two years later, there were more than twenty-five hundred persons—pupils, teachers, employés, and pensioners—in his various establishments.

His seminary for teachers was probably the first distinct Normal school ever established. His orphan school, though perhaps not the first, for one at Rome claims an earlier date, was yet the most successful, and the model of most which have since been established. His instruction, though thorough in the studies undertaken, gave more predominance to moral culture, and to physical science, than to the ancient classics. Latin was carefully and well taught; but in Greek, the New Testament was the only text-book; and Hebrew was one of the studies of the regular course.

The deportment of his students, serious, grave, and temperate, was in marked, perhaps too marked, contrast with that of the students of the other German gymnasia and universities. The necessity of a change of heart, upon which he insisted, for successful scholarship, though resulting, on his part, from his deep religious convictions, yet led, in the course of time, to a degree of Phariseeism and hypocrisy which, for some years, greatly injured the reputation of his schools ; but important reforms and a more liberal course of education have, of late years, restored to them their ancient renown. In his seminary for teachers, in his strictly moral and religious instruction, in the general arrangements and classification of his schools, and in his school-houses—well located, well ventilated, spacious, and convenient—he certainly conferred as great services on the cause of education as any man of the seventeenth century.

Among his collaborators, several attained a high reputation; especially Rambach, author of a treatise on pedagogy, entitled "The Well-instructed Teacher;" Freyer, whose classical works are still in use in Germany; Sarganeck, author of a work on school vices; Hoffmann, author of treatises on natural history for schools; Busching, equally celebrated as a teacher and pedagogical writer; and Steinmetz, who attained renown both as a teacher and preacher.

CHAPTER XIX.

Progress of education in the New England colonies, in the seventeenth century.—Legal provision for the establishment of schools and colleges in Massachusetts and Connecticut.—Legislation of New York for the same end.—Other colonies.—Scotland the first country in Europe to establish a system of common schools.—De la Salle and the Brothers of the Christian Schools.—Statistics of these schools in 1856.

WHILE the efforts of these and other eminent teachers in Europe, were directed to the improvement of education in their respective countries, the colonies which, in 1620 and the twenty-five years succeeding, had left England and planted themselves on the rugged shores of New England, had brought with them not only the manners, customs, and culture of their native land, but the determination to rear here educational institutions which should prevent their descendants from subsiding into barbarism.

Ere their own dwellings were so far completed as to protect them from the inclemency of the climate, they reared the church edifice, and close by its side the school-house, where often, especially in the earlier days of the colonies, men taught the alphabet and the rudiments of learning, whose talents and attainments would have qualified them to fill the highest chair in any university in Europe.

Legal provision was made, in Massachusetts and Connecticut, for the elementary instruction of all the children of each colony, many years before any such enactment had been thought of by any State in Europe. As early as 1635, the formation of free schools was recognized by law in Massachusetts; in 1642, it was ordered, by the General Assembly, that every village, containing fifty families, should maintain a school, in which reading and writing should be taught; and that every township or district, containing one hundred families, should support a grammar-school—*i. e.*, a school where Latin and Greek should be taught. Nor was Connecticut behind her sister colony in her zeal for public and universal education: in 1639, a school supported by tax existed in Hartford, and another in New Haven; and the code of 1650, the first compilation of the laws of the Connecticut commonwealth, required parents and guardians to cause their children to be taught to read, and to learn the catechism, "under a penalty of twenty shillings for each neglect therein;" and authorized the selectmen, after admonition, to take children who were uninstructed, from their parents and guardians, and place them in school.

The same code provided, as in Massachusetts, for the establishment of a school for every fifty householders, and a grammar-school for every hundred householders. In the colony of New Haven, which, until 1665, maintained a separate existence, similar enactments were made, about the same period. Nor were these colonies unmindful of a higher intellectual culture. In 1636, the colony of Massachusetts appropriated £400 for the founding of a college, to which John Harvard, who died in 1638, added about £800 more, and thus secured the establishment, within eighteen years after the first settlers landed upon Plymouth Rock, of a college whose reputation has constantly increased from that day to this. In the support of this seat of learning, the Plymouth, Connecticut, and New Haven colonies all contributed according to their ability.

In 1700, though impoverished by repeated Indian wars, the colonies of Connecticut and New Haven, at this time united under a single government, considering the interests of education and religion as requiring the founding of another college, determined upon establishing one at Saybrook (subsequently removed to New Haven), and granted it, from the colonial treasury, an annuity of £60 sterling.

In the other English colonies, the progress of education was less rapid. Schools were established, for those who had the means to pay for tuition, in New Amsterdam (New York), under the Dutch administration, in 1633, and at Beaverwyck (Albany), in 1642; and the Dutch West India Company subsequently sent out, from Holland, teachers for all the settlements.

In 1687, a Latin school was opened, in the city of New York, under the sanction of the English government; but the colonial government did not provide for education till 1702, when a grammar-school was established, by the legislature, and £50 per annum appropriated, for seven years, for the support of a teacher. In Pennsylvania, Virginia, and the Carolinas, but little was done, during the seventeenth century, for education. A few schools were established for the children of the wealthier planters, but no general system of instruction prevailed.

The first country in Europe to establish a complete system of parish-schools, for the instruction of all the children of the country, was Scotland. By an enactment, in 1696, it was provided that every parish should maintain a school, with a male teacher, for whom the landholders should erect a school-house and a dwelling. It has resulted from this enactment that, at this day, the people of Scotland, of all classes, are more intelligent and better educated than those of any other country of Europe, with the possible exception of Prussia.

Before closing our account of education in the seventeenth century, we must say a few words of the order of *Brothers of the Christian Schools*, founded by Jean Baptist de la Salle, at Rheims in 1679, and at Paris in 1688, though not attaining to any considerable distinction until the earlier years of the eighteenth century. De la Salle was a philanthropist, in the best sense of that term. Deeply impressed with the necessity of bestowing a better education on the children of the poorer classes, he devoted his patrimony and his entire life and labors to the work, and organized this order, as the best method, in his judgment, of promoting an object he had so much at heart.

Before intrusting the Brothers with the charge of schools, they were required to pass through a novitiate, somewhat like the normal schools of more modern times. At first, he required that their instruction should be gratuitous; but subsequently, the members of the order were so much in demand, as teachers, that they were allowed to receive salaries, accounting for all their receipts, except their frugal fare, to their superiors in the order. The members of this order form the largest proportion of the professional teachers of the Roman Catholic Church. In 1856, they reported eight hundred and seventy-one schools, attended by about three hundred thousand children.

CHAPTER XX.

The Humanists, and their system of instruction.—Eminent Humanist teachers.—J. J. Rousseau.—Influence of his "*Emile*" upon education.—John Locke.—John B. Basedow.—His early career.—The "*Elementar-Werk.*"—The *Philanthropinum.*—Small success of his personal teachings.—The impulse given to education by his efforts. —*Wölke* and the other successors of Basedow.—Count Zinzendorf. —Humanitarian institutions devoted to the education of the deaf and dumb, the blind, juvenile offenders, &c.—Special schools of commerce, &c.—Eminent German writers on education.

Somewhat later in date, though in part cotemporaneous with the *pietistic* school of teachers, were the *Humanists*, so named because they, in opposition to the Pietists, insisted upon a more thorough classical culture, the study of the *humanities*, as the instruction in the classics was termed. Cellarius, one of the most eminent of these teachers, whose contributions to school literature, in the way of Latin and Greek text-books, are worthy of record, was the cotemporary of Spener and Francke; J. M. Gesner (1691–1761), professor successively at Weimar, Jena, Leipsic, and

Gottingen, founder of the pedagogical seminary at Gottingen, and author of more than thirty educational works, was not only a man of almost universal scholarship, but also a wise and judicious teacher; Ernesti (1733–1801), nearly as profound in attainments, lived almost wholly in antiquity, and, by his zeal in antiquarian investigation, exerted a powerful influence on his pupils.

Heyne (1729–1812), perhaps the finest classical scholar of modern times, by his excellent editions of the classics, by his direction of the School of Ilefeld, and finally by his labors in the University of Gottingen, where some of the most profound linguists of the age were educated, exerted a beneficial influence upon thousands of the youth of Germany. Jacobs and Creuzer, although following in the same course, belong rather to the present than the eighteenth century, and will be noticed further on. Meantime, Jean Jacques Rousseau (1712–1778), a man who, if his own confessions may be believed, was any thing but exemplary in his character, had, by his pedagogical works, opened the way for the establishment of a new system of teaching, which, for many years, exerted a powerful influence in Germany.

The *Emile* of Rousseau, the work of a man who had never taught, and of a father who had sent his own children, at birth, to the Foundling Hospital, contained some pedagogical truth, mixed with much of sophistry, falsehood, and immorality. Its pretence of following nature awakened the minds of some better men to a consideration of the natural methods of instruction.

The educational works of John Locke, to whom we have already referred, also exerted some influence in turning the attention of teachers to nature, as a safe guide in the matter of education. Locke, like Rousseau, was a theorist; but, unlike him, his instincts and sympathies were on the side of morality and virtue.

John Bernhard Basedow (1723–1790), a man of but limited education and little refinement, yet energetic, bold, self-reliant, and of great firmness and perseverance, after a somewhat singular career, in which he had been almost constantly engaged in theological controversies, published in 1768, in his forty-fifth year, a prospectus of an "Elementary Book of Human Knowledge." Assisted by an allowance from the Danish minister, Bernstorff, he devoted the next six years to its preparation. It was published in 1774, in four volumes, with one hundred plates. Its plan contemplated, — 1. Elementary instruction in the knowledge of words and things; 2. A method of teaching children to read, without weariness or loss of time; 3. Natural knowledge; 4. Knowledge of morals, the mind, and reasoning; 5. Natural religion; 6. A knowledge of social duties, commerce, &c. Covering nearly the same ground with the celebrated work of Comenius, this *Elementar-Werk* might well be called the *Orbis Pictus* of the eighteenth century. His system of instruction thus published, he was soon summoned to put it in practice; which he did, at Dessau, by the aid of Prince Leopold of Anhalt-Dessau, by the foundation of his *Philanthropinum*, an institution in which nature was to be followed in the plan of education. All nations were to participate in its advantages, on equal terms; and a creed, so general that even deists could subscribe to it, was to take the place of religious instruction.

The number of pupils, at first, was small, only thirteen being in attendance at the end of two years. In 1776, Basedow issued a boastful and pompous circular, promising the most extraordinary results from his new method, and inviting princes, nobles, and others to attend his examinations, some three months later; the reports of this examination led to some increase of pupils, though the number was never very great. In 1778, Basedow left the Philanthropinum, and Wölke, previously his assistant, and a man of much greater ability than Basedow, became the principal. Basedow, whose latter years were clouded by intemperance and a morose temper, taught privately at Dessau, and published some of his later pedagogical works there.

The Philanthropinum flourished for a while, under the care of Wölke and his able assistants, Salzmann, Campé, and others; but was finally closed, in 1793, having, however, led to the institution of other schools on the same system, in Marschlius, Switzerland, and in Hamburg, St. Petersburg, Durkheim, and Schnepfenthal. The last, founded by Salzmann, in 1784, still exists.

Philanthropism, as the theory of Basedow was called, though an imperfect system of education, yet accomplished something for its improvement. It led to a better appreciation of the necessity of physical training, to greater activity of the reflective faculties, liberated the reasoning faculties from the thraldom of the scholastic philosophy, and abolished the terrible cruelties of the old school discipline. It prepared the way, also, for other and better systems of instruction, which were soon to follow. Many of its teachers distinguished themselves, also, by their writings on the subject of education. Wölke, Gutsmuth, Salzmann, Campé, Rochow, Becker, Schweighauser, and Trapp made valuable contributions to the school literature of the age.

Another zealous and efficient patron of education, though belonging wholly to the eighteenth century, is rather to be ranked among the Pietists than the Philanthropists in his principles—Count Zinzendorf (1700–1760), the restorer of the sect of *Moravians*, a pupil of Francke, established, in Europe and America, numerous schools, modeled after those at Halle; and, through the impulse which he gave to education among his followers, led indirectly to the founding of many others, most of which still exist.

The strife which raged between the Pietists, the Humanists, and the Philanthropists, led many eminent friends of education to stand aloof from each of these schools, and to labor for the promotion of learning on wider and less exclusive principles. Some of these, impelled by a truly philanthropic spirit, sought out classes hitherto neglected, and endeavored to instruct them: such was the origin of the efforts for the instruction of deaf mutes, by Heinicke, Braidwood, the Abbé De l'Epée, and Sicard; the instruction of the blind, by Valentin Haüy, Klein, and Zeuné; the establishment of Sunday-schools by Vincent de Paul, Robert Raikes, Fox, and Oberlin; the organization of Reformatories by Odescalchi and Tata Giovanni at Rome, and the Philanthropic Society at London.

Such, too, was the origin of many of those special schools of commerce, agriculture, mines, the arts of design, &c.

Many of these *eclectic* teachers, as Fritz and others have named them, have also contributed materially to the advancement of education by their works. In Germany particularly, which, during the latter part of the eighteenth century, was the theater of the most active discussion of the principles of education, *Sulzer*, author of a work "*On the Education of Children*," and a "*Resumé of the Sciences*;" *Miller*, whose "*Principles of a Wise and Christian Instruction*" and "*Moral Pictures*" are still popular; *Bock*, and KANT, the celebrated philosopher, both of whom wrote manuals of pedagogics; *Weisse*, whose "*Friend of Children*" is still a favorite with both children and parents; *Ehlers*, whose "*Directions for Princes and the Governors of Princes*" show a profound knowledge of the principles of education; *Büsch*, the founder of the first school of commerce, at Hamburg, in 1775, and a thoroughly practical writer; *Feder*, the able antagonist of Rousseau, and author of the *New Emile; Resewitz*, the accomplished director of the Klosterbergen Gymnasium, whose "*Educational Thoughts, Projects, and Directions*," and "*Education of the Citizen*," contain more valuable thoughts and suggestions for the teacher than any other work of the last century; *Gurlitt*, the distinguished director of the gymnasium at Hamburg, author of numerous small works on education, and *Rœtger*, *Heusinger*, *A. H. Niemeyer*, *Schwartz*, and *Beneke*—all able writers, but belonging rather to the present century than the last—have furnished, by their works, valuable additions both to the theoretical and practical knowledge of the art of instruction.

CHAPTER XXI.

PESTALOZZI.—Abstract of his views on education, as developed in his works.—Objections to some of his positions.—His own imperfect success as a teacher.—Prevalence of the Pestalozzian system at the present day.—Other educational reformers cotemporary with Pestalozzi.—Fellenberg, Jacotot, Felbiger, Father Girard, and Lancaster. —Review of their several methods.—Adoption of the method of Sagan, introduced by Felbiger, in Austria.—The Lancasterian system.—At one time prevalent in England and America.—Its defects. —The labors of Oberlin, the brothers Zeller, Vehrli, and Wichern, in promoting education.—Cheering prospects of the future.

THE man who has exerted the most influence over the education of the race, in the last hundred years, is J. H. PESTALOZZI (1746–1827). Like Basedow, his own education was imperfect and one-sided; like him, he had read, and was greatly impressed by Rousseau's *Emile;* like him, too, he was visionary and extravagant in his hopes and expectations, and even to a much greater degree than Basedow himself; but, unlike him, he was a man of warm and loving heart, of high and pure aspirations, and of a deeply religious spirit.

His life, judged as men ordinarily judge, was a series of failures; he lacked practical talent and tact: nothing to which he put his hand prospered, or, if it seemed to do so for a time, the seeds of decay and destruction were early sown in it, and it soon went to ruin. None felt this more, or were more deeply humbled by it, than himself; yet, with all this want of direct success, he initiated a great and successful educational movement, which is, this day, bearing fruit in the intellectual culture and advancement of millions.

An influence so extensive, demands from us a brief examination of the principles on which his system was founded, its excellencies, and defects. His fundamental principle, as developed in his "*Leonard and Gertrude*," his "*How Gertrude teaches her Children*," and his "*Book for Mothers*," was that education should proceed according to the laws of nature; that it was the duty of the teacher to assist this, by exciting the child to self-activity, and rendering him only a limited degree of assistance; that progress should be slow and gradual, but uninterrupted, never passing to a second topic till the first is fully understood; that the memory and the understanding should not be unduly cultivated, but all the faculties developed in harmony; that the peculiarities of every child and of each sex should be carefully studied, in order to adapt instruction to them; that the elements of all knowledge were Form, Number, and Language, and that these elements should be taught with simplicity and thoroughness; that the art of observing should be acquired, and the perceptive faculties well developed; that every topic of instruction should become an exercise for the reflective powers; that mental arithmetic, geometry, and the arts of drawing and modeling objects of beauty, were all important exercises for training, strengthening, and disciplining the mind; that the laws of language should be developed from within, and the exercises in it made not only to cultivate the intellect, but to improve the affections; that vocal music should be taught in schools, not by rote, but by a careful study of the elementary principles of music; that the

Socratic method, as used by Basedow and others, was objectionable, and that, in the early stages of instruction, dictation by the teacher and repetition by the scholar is preferable, and, at a more advanced stage, the giving out problems by the teacher, to be solved by the pupil, without assistance; that religious instruction should begin with the mother, that the filial feelings of the child should be first cultivated, and directed toward God, and that formal religious instruction should be reserved to a later period, when the child can understand it; that despotic and cruel government in schools was improper, but that mutual affection between teacher and pupil was a better incitement to intellectual activity than prizes, or other stimulants to emulation; and, finally, that the exercise of the senses and the thorough cultivation of the physical powers, were of very great importance to the complete development of the child.

Most of these principles were excellent, and many of them greatly in advance of any previous system; but the practical defects were, that though the intellect was quickened, there was too little positive knowledge communicated; that excessive attention was given to mathematical and intuitive studies, to the neglect of other branches of knowledge; that simplification was carried too far, and continued too long; that too little attention was given to historical truth, and to testimony as a source of knowledge, especially in matters of religion; and that he fell too much into Basedow's error, of regarding religious knowledge as innate.

Pestalozzi's principles were, however, better than his practice, and in other hands accomplished more than in his own. The system of instruction which, in the Prussian schools, has been so successful in the intellectual development of the nation, is based on that of Pestalozzi, with but few and slight modifications; and in England and our own country, as well as in the North of Europe, his method has exerted a more powerful influence on teachers than any other.

Several cotemporaries of Pestalozzi have

also distinguished themselves by systems or methods of instruction, which have exerted a wide, and, in some countries, a controlling influence. Prominent among these, are Fellenberg, Jacotot, Felbiger, Father Girard, and Lancaster.

Fellenberg (1771–1844) was, like Pestalozzi, a Swiss, but, unlike him, a man of rank and fortune. He devoted himself and his fortune to the establishment of an institution at Hofwyl, a few miles from Berne, which comprised an agricultural institute, theoretical and practical; a manufactory of agricultural implements and machines; a rural school for the poor, in which they were taught the principles of agriculture, in connection with other studies; a superior school, for the education of the young nobility of Germany; an intermediate school, for the training of the middle classes; and a normal school, for the instruction of the teachers of the canton. His system was in many respects analogous to that of Pestalozzi, but was preferable to it, in that it communicated more positive knowledge, was more practical in character, maintained a more just equipoise of the faculties, and gave more weight to historic truth, and to the revelation of the Holy Scriptures. His schools were discontinued in 1848, except the Poor-school, the pupils of which are employed in practical agriculture on his large estate.

Jacotot (1770–1840) was a native of France, educated at Dijon, and subsequently a professor in the University of Louvain. His method, which has been very generally adopted in Belgium, and to some extent in other countries, was intended to give more exercise to the memorizing faculty than the Pestalozzian school had done. He required his pupils to commit all the lessons to memory, whether in the languages or sciences, and the teacher explained briefly any difficulty; the next day they were to repeat the same lesson, and give an explanation of it themselves;—this, he contended, gave them more command of language, more positive knowledge, and greater power of using it, than the method of Pestalozzi.

Felbiger, an Austrian bishop of Sagan, in Silesia, and subsequently (not far from 1770) appointed director-general of the Austrian schools, was the author of the *Method of Sagan*, named in honor of his former see. Felbiger had, previous to assuming the office of director-general, traveled extensively over Europe, investigating the different systems of education, and ascertaining their practical value. On his return, he organized, at first in Silesia, and afterward in other parts of Austria, normal schools, and primary and secondary schools, and procured the passage of a law requiring parents to send their children to school, under the penalty of fines and corporal punishment.

The teachers were all examined, and the schools required to be taught, according to the Method of Sagan—a combination of the methods of Basedow and Pestalozzi. Every thing taught was regarded in a merely practical and utilitarian view; the teacher proceeded from the known to the unknown with great rapidity, and it was to be his aim to develop the intelligence rather than the memory. Instruction was given on the simultaneous system; the classes were carefully formed with reference to the progress and talents of the pupils who composed them, and frequent examinations tested their improvement.

The system, though faulty, was very well adapted for schools where the teachers and scholars were regarded as mere machines; and it is not surprising that it was universally adopted in Austria. In Bohemia, the Method of Sagan was also propagated, by command ot Maria Theresa, by the zealous labors of Kindermann (de Schulstein), a friend and coworker with Felbiger. This system was in vogue throughout the Empire of Austria until the last fifteen years.

Father Girard (1765–1850) was a monk of the order of Cordeliers, a native of Fribourg, Switzerland, a man of a catholic and liberal spirit, and earnestly devoted to the cause of education. He established a school at Fribourg, in which he adopted, with some modifications, the system of Pestalozzi, upon whose labors he had been called by the government to make an examination and report. He regarded the practice of questioning the pupils, after the manner of Basedow, with more favor than Pestalozzi. His school, while enjoying a high reputation, was broken up by the intrigues of the Jesuits. In 1835, he published a valuable work, entitled "*Educational Course in the Maternal Language, for the Use of Schools and Families.*"

Joseph Lancaster (1771–1839) was a native of England, a member of the Society of Friends. He will be remembered by posterity as the founder of the monitorial, or *Lancasterian system*, as it was usually called, in which the most intelligent pupils in a class were required to teach their fellows that which they had acquired.

This plan, it was argued, developed the intellect of the young monitor, and at the same time his intellectual attainments were so nearly on a level with those of his companions, that he would be better able to explain the lesson to their understandings, than a teacher who was very considerably beyond them in knowledge. This system was, theoretically, very plausible, and at one period great numbers of schools, particularly in cities and large towns, both in England and this country, adopted it. It was found, however, that the knowledge of the monitors was, for the most part, crude and confused, and that they oftener taught error than truth; and the system is now generally abandoned. The method was not the invention of Mr. Lancaster, for Pestalozzi had practiced it to some extent, and Trotzendorf, two centuries earlier, also; but it was more fully developed and systematized by him than it had previously been. The latter years of his life, from 1818 to his death, were spent in this country.

Among those who have, by their humble but assiduous labors in the cause of the education of the poor, exerted a powerful influence in the promotion of universal education, we should mention, also, the pastor *Oberlin*, of the Ban de la Roche (1740–1826), by whose zeal and patience the half-savage population of that sterile mountain district were changed into an intelligent, hospitable, refined, and happy people; the brothers *Zeller*, who, in their several capacities—the elder as high-school councilor of Prussia, and the younger as superintendent of the seminary for orphan and destitute children, and teachers of the poor, at Beuggen—have accomplished much for the education of the lower classes; and *Jacob Vehrli*, for fifty years at the head of the normal school for country teachers at Kruitzlingen, from whence he has sent forth an influence for good over Switzerland, Germany, France, and England.

Humanitarian education has made very great progress, during the last seventy years, in Europe as well as in the United States. There are now nearly or quite two hundred institutions for deaf mutes, more than one hundred for the blind, about twenty for idiots, and more than five hundred for juvenile vagrants and offenders.

In the reformatory schools, *Dr. J. H. Wichern*, of Horn, near Hamburg; *MM. De Metz* and *Bretigneres de Courteilles*, at Mettray; *MM. Ducpetiaux*, at Brussels, and *Pol*, at Ruysselede; and *Messrs. Turner*, *Giles*, *Lloyd Baker*, and others, in England, are deserving of special notice.

In this country, the humanitarian institutions are numerous, and better conducted than in Europe, except those for reformatory education, where the evils of the congregated system have prevented, to some extent, that progress which is desirable.

The present condition of education throughout the civilized world is hopeful: intelligence is more generally diffused than at any previous period of the world's history; every branch of science has received new impulses within the past sixty years; the subjects of knowledge are constantly extending, the discoveries in physical science have opened a new world to the dominion of man; philology and its cognate sciences have been greatly extended, the topics and methods of study have been increased and enlarged; the press has become, not the third or fourth, but the *first* power in the State; newspapers, which, prior to the present century, had but few readers, and exerted comparatively little influence, now visit almost every household, and influence the views and opinions of men, to a greater extent than any other agency. The progress of moral education has, on the whole, fully kept pace with intellectual culture. Physical training is not yet sufficiently practiced, but material progress is making in this particular.

CHAPTER XXII.

Review of the present condition of education in the principal countries of the world.—England.—Scotland, Ireland, France, Spain, and Portugal.—The States of the Church, Sardinia, Tuscany, Naples, Turkey, Greece, Russia, Lapland, and Finmark.—Norway, Sweden, and Denmark.

A BRIEF review of the present condition of education in the more prominent countries of the world, and statistics concerning the number under instruction, may fitly close our brief history. In ENGLAND, the facilities for acquiring a thorough university education are excellent, for those who have sufficient means at command; the course of study at Cambridge and Oxford, though perhaps giving excessive prominence to classical and mathematical studies, is still well calculated to develop the intellectual powers. The London University, and some of the colleges of the dissenters, give more attention to physical science. The great endowed schools of Eton, Rugby, Harrow, Westminster, Winchester, Christ's Hospital, &c., &c., are, for the most part, devoted to classical and mathematical training.

In provision for the education of the masses, England is yet far behind many of the countries of Europe. The great difficulty has been a religious one,—the so-called national schools, as well as most others which received assistance from the government, being under the control of the Established Church, and the children of dissenters being educated in private schools. Still, under the persevering efforts of Lord Brougham, Sir J. Kay Shuttleworth, the Earl of Shaftesbury, Lord Stanley, and other distinguished friends of education, there has been decisive progress within a few years past: the factory children are not now brought up in utter ignorance; a cheap yet instructive literature pervades every hamlet, and has developed, even in the lowest classes, a love of reading; evening schools for adults, and Sunday-schools, which there, as well as on the continent, are very often occupied with instruction in reading and other elementary branches, are very largely attended.

The education of deaf mutes and the blind, is more limited than in France or this country, being generally confined to reading, writing, and the acquisition of some mechanical art, on the part of the deaf and dumb; and reading by touch, singing, playing on musical instruments, and knitting, mat-braiding, weaving, or basket-making, for the blind.

The Reformatories of England are deserving of high praise, both for their number and success. Hundreds are every year rescued by them from a life of crime, and rendered good and intelligent citizens.

SCOTLAND is inferior to England in its facilities for higher education; and the low salaries afforded to the professors in its universities, prevent, in many cases, highly qualified scholars from accepting the posts; but in secondary and primary education, it is far in advance of England. Its system of parish-schools is not, indeed, perfect, but it is constantly improving. Its humanitarian institutions have a higher reputation than those south of the Tweed.

IRELAND, so long the victim of ignorance

and misrule, is improving in education and general intelligence, as much, or more than any country of Europe. Within a few years, good schools have been greatly multiplied; and, ere long, her peasantry will be beyond those of England in intelligence. This is the result of the system of national education, established there about thirty years since, which, from small beginnings, and the constant and violent opposition of ultraists among both Protestants and Catholics, has at last drawn into its schools the great bulk of the children of the country. It provides for *combined* secular, and *separate* religious instruction, and thus obviates the great difficulties under which the English schools have labored.

In FRANCE, *superior education*, as it is called, especially in mathematical and physical science, is not inferior to that of any country in the world; and the colleges and lyceums which are found in every considerable town in the empire, are generally well conducted. In thorough classical knowledge, we doubt if the French scholars are equal to the Germans, and in *belles-lettres* they are certainly not superior to the English. In philosophy they have many illustrious names.

Primary education was very much neglected from the time of the Revolution of 1793 to the accession of Louis Philippe; but the efforts of that monarch, seconded, most zealously, by Guizot, effected, in the course of the next eighteen years, a wonderful change; and, in 1850, only two thousand five hundred communes, out of more than thirty-eight thousand, were without one or more primary schools, and one-ninth of the whole population were attending school. The instruction in these primary schools might be improved; in too many of them the method of Jacotot, or that of the Brothers of the Christian Schools, in which too much reliance is placed on the memory, and the understanding is not sufficiently cultivated, are practiced. The charitable, reformatory, and special schools of France are generally well conducted, and the success of some of them—that of the institutes for the deaf and dumb, and for the blind, and the reformatory colony at Mettray—has been been such as to attract the attention of all the nations of Europe.

Of the educational condition of SPAIN and PORTUGAL, we cannot speak so favorably. Harassed, for years, by internal discords and civil wars, the glory which once belonged to their universities has long since departed; even the children of the wealthy and noble are but indifferently taught, and the offspring of the poor seldom find any other school than that at their own fireside. The rigid adherence of the people to the Catholic faith, has prevented the introduction (once attempted) of more modern systems of instruction, like that of Pestalozzi; and the methods of the Jesuits and the Esculapians (an order similar to the Brothers of the Christian Schools), and even the still older systems of the middle ages, characterize the teachings of the secondary and primary schools, while the scholastic philosophy still finds a home within the walls of her universities.

In ITALY, the STATES OF THE CHURCH do not

lack for schools or colleges. Education is superintended by a company of cardinals, who, under the designation of the *Congregation of Studies*, make the examinations, and, personally or by deputy, appoint the professors and teachers. The primary or communal schools are under the immediate supervision of the bishops, who are also generally chancellors of the universities. There are also regional schools, and schools for each sex, under the direction of several of the religious orders. Most of these schools are free, or nearly so, in many of them the teachers being supported by endowments.

The instruction, in most of them, is not very thorough, except on religious topics; and the old memorizing system is in vogue. The standard of education in the universities and colleges is not high; and these States, which, at the revival of learning, produced some of the most eminent scholars of Europe, have now but little literary reputation.

SARDINIA, which, up to 1848, was behind most of the other countries of Europe in education, has, since that time, almost taken its place among the foremost. This is due, in part, to the labors of Antonio Rosmini, an accomplished educator, and writer on pedagogical science; and in part to the impulse given to the nation by a constitutional government and their emancipation from priestly influence.

The system of education embraces superior and inferior primary schools, for all the children of the kingdom; secondary schools, colleges, universities, and special schools; the Pestalozzian method is generally adopted, and normal schools, well conducted, are fast supplying competent teachers. With better textbooks, and a few years' experience in her present system, the population of Sardinia will speedily become one of the most intelligent in Southern Europe.

TUSCANY, under Austrian influence, has adopted, to a considerable extent, the Austrian system of education; her schools are, for the most part, in good repute, and the Universities of Pisa and Sierra retain something of their ancient renown. Relatively, however, to the other countries of Europe, Tuscany has fallen much from its old position. The home of the Medicis, the birth-place of Dante, of Lionardo da Vinci, and of numerous others of the noblest names of Italy, it once stood in the front rank among the intelligent and educated nations of Christendom; but now its presses are controlled by the censorship, and its universities graduate few men of distinction.

The Kingdom of Naples, or the Two Sicilies, is in a very low educational condition. Sicily has more schools than the continental portion of the kingdom, but they are not well conducted, and beyond reading and writing, the children make very little progress. Its colleges and universities have some reputation, but the despotic character of the government is unfavorable to much intellectual freedom or activity.

Turkey has schools for its Moslem population, and its laws make it obligatory on every parent to send his children to school. The teaching is in Turkish and Arabic, and is not generally of the highest order; there has been, however, material improvement since 1847, when a system of intermediate schools was established, which took the place of the secondary schools of other countries. Previously there had only existed the *mekteb*, or elementary schools, and the *medressehs*, or gymnasia. There are some special schools, but education is at a low ebb.

GREECE has, since its independence, made zealous efforts for the improvement of public instruction. There is an efficient university at Athens, secondary schools in each considerable town, and, in most cases, elementary schools in each commune. The Pestalozzian system is generally adopted. As yet, however, not much more than one-fourth of the children are under instruction.

RUSSIA, though in many respects only a semi-civilized nation, has made very strenuous exertions, of late years, to improve the educational condition of its people. Its universities and its special schools of military, mining, engineering, manufacturing, and agricultural science, are worthy of very high commendation for the extent and thoroughness of their instruction. Provision is made for the elementary instruction of the children of the soldiery, who are generally expected to follow their fathers' profession; but, although *ukases* have been issued, ordering the establishment of schools in every commune, yet not one-seventh of the children of European Russia receive any instruction whatever. The present Czar is deeply interested in the improvement of the social and intellectual condition of his people, and his efforts will not be wanting to effect a favorable progress in this direction.

LAPLAND and FINMARK are almost destitute of schools, though many of the Lapps and Fins acquire a knowledge of reading, and some of them have become eminent as scholars. The people of Iceland are generally intelligent, but their education is, for the most part, domestic, or communicated by their pastors.

In NORWAY, though the sparseness of the population is a great drawback to the maintenance of good schools in the country, education is very general. Only about one-eighth of her population dwell in towns. For these, the advantages of education are hardly surpassed by any country in Europe: there are elementary and upper district-schools, citizens' schools, answering very nearly to our academies; Real schools, in which technical science is taught in connection with the knowledge of modern languages; Latin or cathedral schools, furnishing a classical education; military, agricultural, drawing, and polytechnic schools; normal schools, and a university. In the country, there are what are called *ambulatory schools*, kept by teachers who go from hamlet to hamlet, and teach for about eight weeks in each.

In SWEDEN, education is very general. Through the efforts of Mr. Siljeström, a law has been passed, requiring at least one stationary school in each parish, and normal schools for teachers, in addition to the ambulatory schools, which are still necessary in the districts of scattered and sparse population. The system of schools is quite complete, but the quality of the teaching is susceptible of improvement. In physical education the Swedes are not equaled by any country in Europe. Their universities at Upsala and Lund have a high reputation.

DENMARK has for many years maintained a high standard of education; the proportion of pupils in school to the whole population, is said to be greater than that of any other country in Europe. The Pestalozzian method is generally adopted; and there is a complete system of graded schools, from the university to the primary school.

CHAPTER XXIII.

The German States.—Prussia, Saxony, and Wurtemberg.—Austria, Bohemia, Croatia, and the Austrian Archduchies in Italy.—Bavaria, Mecklenburg, and the smaller States.—Eminent living and recent German writers on education.—AFRICA.—Egypt and the tributaries of the Porte.—Algiers, Sierra Leone, Liberia, Cape Colony.—Other portions of the African continent.—ASIA.—Persia, Independent and Chinese Tartary, Afghanistan and Beloochistan, Siberia, China, and Japan.—Thibet, Siam, Tonquin, Burmah, Malacca, The Karens and Shyens, India, Australia, New Zealand, and the Pacific islands.

THE States of Germany, with hardly an exception, occupy a high educational position. There is, however, a difference in these States. Prussia, Saxony, and Wurtemberg are perhaps entitled to the first rank, Austria to the second, and Bavaria, Mecklenburg, and perhaps some other of the smaller States to the lowest. In PRUSSIA, as well as in several of the other German States, a modification of the Pestalozzian method is adopted. The elementary text-book in the primary schools, is a Reader (a modern *Orbis Pictus*), in which the rudiments of geography (the geography of Germany), natural history, arithmetic, language, &c., are arranged as reading lessons; and all instruction not found in the Reader, is communicated orally by the teacher, assisted, however, by maps, drawings, specimens of natural history, &c., which are found in every schoolroom.

Eight years' attendance upon the schools is compulsory upon the children; they pass from the primary to the burgher schools, the Real schools, the gymnasia, and the university, if they choose to obtain a thorough education. Prussia abounds in special schools. There are advantages of higher education open to females. Normal schools are established in all the principal towns of the kingdom; but the demand for teachers is so much greater than the supply, that, in 1854, the period of training was shortened, and the standard of attainments lowered,—a measure regarded by eminent educators as extremely injurious to the welfare of the schools. The plan of education adopted in SAXONY and WURTEMBERG, differs but little from that of Prussia. It is perhaps somewhat more thorough and liberal in Saxony, and its results are highly satisfactory.

AUSTRIA, though far behind Prussia and several of the other States in intellectual progress, is improving. Austria proper has, within a few years, made great advance in her elementary schools, and has established many *Real* schools, which differ from those bearing the same name in North Germany, in being more technical in their character, and in pursuing a more extended course. The *Method of Sagan* has given place to better systems of instruction; and though there is still great room for improvement, yet Austria occupies a very fair position among the countries of Europe in the intelligence of its people.

Since 1855, attendance upon the schools has been made compulsory; and great efforts have been made to extend to Hungary, Bohemia, Croatia, and Austrian Italy similar regulations to those maintained in the Archduchy of Austria.

In BAVARIA, Mecklenburg, and some of the

other small German States, the governments have taken less interest in the promotion of education than in the States already named, and the schools, consequently, have not attained a high position. Higher education is, however, well cared for in Bavaria, and the fine arts are cultivated, at Munich, with a zeal unsurpassed in Germany.

The present generation has not been without able pedagogical writers in Germany. Von Raumer, Diesterweg, Blochmann, Niemeyer, and Schwarz have rendered good service to the work of instruction by their works on the history and science of pedagogy.

In the variety and extent of their charitable educational institutions, the Germans have surpassed all the other nations of Europe. They have a great number of institutions for the deaf and dumb, ten or twelve for the blind, two for idiots, and four or five for cretins; *crechés* and *kinder-garten* (children's gardens), for infants; some hundreds of reformatories, for all classes of juvenile offenders and vagrants; orphan schools, almost without number; industrial schools; "work schools," for pauper children, one of which, that of Gustavus Werner at Reutlingen, has in training and supervision seven hundred pauper children; schools for the education and training of deaconesses, or Protestant sisters of charity, hospital nurses and superintendents,—like that of Pastor Fliedner, at Kaiserswerth, where Florence Nightingale received the instruction which qualified her for her noble work; the schools of the Inner Mission, at Horn, near Hamburg, where young men are trained to take charge of reformatories, prisons, hospitals, &c.;—in short, the comprehensive German heart has, it would seem, provided institutions to meet all the ills, the wants, and deficiencies of suffering and sinful humanity.

On the great African continent, we find but little attention paid to education. EGYPT and the TRIBUTARIES OF THE PORTE, in Northern Africa, have schools after the Moslem fashion, in which the children of the true believers are taught to read the Koran, and acquire a little rudimentary knowledge of arithmetic. ALGIERS, as a French colony, is receiving the French system of communal and higher schools. The English and American settlements at SIERRA LEONE and LIBERIA have established schools in accordance with the plans of the mother countries, Liberia having organized also a college. The CAPE COLONY has free schools in every district, and two colleges; but the vast territories which comprise the interior, and eastern coast of the continent, can hardly be said to have any system of education.

Those tribes and countries into which the Arabs have penetrated, have usually a few persons who can read and write; and in the Portuguese settlements, which occasionally dot the coasts, may be found some persons of Portuguese extraction, who possess a tolerable education;—but aside from these, and the few schools which the missionaries have been able to establish at their various stations, there is nothing which can, in the ordinary sense of the term, be called education.

Portions of Asia are less degraded. In PERSIA there still remains the tradition of the learning which once made Bagdad and Ispahan the centers of intelligence for the worshipers of Mohammed; and many of the Persian *mullahs* are, at the present day, accomplished in the Arabic lore, which was so highly prized in the days of the Abassides.

Further east, the nomadic tribes which roam over the wide *steppes* of INDEPENDENT and CHINESE TARTARY, and the thievish, freebooting AFGHANS and BELOOCHEES, have little respect for books or learning. The principal towns of SIBERIA have schools and educated people; but they are exiles from Russia, or officers and their families who are located there on duty.

Of CHINA and JAPAN we have already spoken; their systems of education have changed but little, probably, for two thousand five hundred years. In THIBET, the condition of education does not vary, materially, from that of China. SIAM, TONQUIN, and BURMAH, professing substantially the Büdhist faith, have also the Büdhist educational system; while the inhabitants of MALACCA and the MALAYSIAN ISLES are hardly to be considered as possessing any education.

A large population, extending over considerable portions of Farther India, and known under the names of *Karens* and *Shyens*, have not embraced the Büdhist doctrines, and possessed no written language until they were provided with one by the missionaries.

In INDIA, while the Brahminical system has made small advance from its methods of instruction two thousand years ago, the East India Company have made some efforts to establish colleges for the education of such of the Brahmins as might fill offices in the employ of the Company; and the missionaries of the different denominations have established schools, of different grades, in various parts of India. The mutiny and war have broken up many of these, but they will probably be reopened.

In AUSTRALIA, schools have been established and liberally supported by the government; and two colleges, one at Sydney and the other at Melbourne, have been founded. TASMANIA, NEW ZEALAND, the SOCIETY and the SANDWICH ISLANDS, all have good schools; and, in the two latter groups, the natives are, many of them, acquiring considerable education. At Oahu, one of the Sandwich Islands grou] a college has recently been established.

CHAPTER XXIV.

North and South America.—Canada East and West.—United States. —Northern and Southern States.—Hispano-American States: Mexico, Central America, &c.—West India Islands: Cuba, Porto Rico, Jamaica, Trinidad, Hayti, &c.—South America.—New Grenada, Venezuela, Ecuador.—French, Dutch, and British Guiana.—Brazil, the Argentine Confederation, Buenos Ayres, Uruguay, and Paraguay.—Chile, Bolivia, and Peru.

TURNING our attention to the American continent, we find in NEWFOUNDLAND a low state of education; in NEW BRUNSWICK, a larger number of schools in proportion to the population, and a college, not very efficient; in CANADA EAST, a good school system, embracing all grades from the university to the primary school, and an annually increasing attendance and efficiency; in CANADA WEST, an organization unsurpassed in its results, for attendance and intellectual progress, by any in the world.

In the UNITED STATES there is a great variety in the educational condition of different sections of the country. The Northern States, owing in part to their more compact population, and in part also to the strong conviction of the necessity of popular education, received from the large infusion of settlers of New England birth, have generally efficient school-systems; and though, in some of them, owing to the very recent period of their settlement, the details are not yet thoroughly wrought out, yet they can not fail, in a few years, to present a condition, in respect to education, unequaled by any nation on the globe.

The Southern States, on the other hand, owing to the sparseness of their inhabitants, the existence of a large servile population, and the wealth of the principal property-holders, have not generally attained to so high an educational position.

A few of these States have made praiseworthy efforts for a more effective school-system, and, considering the difficulties with which they have had to contend, have made good progress; among these, North Carolina, Alabama, Missouri, Kentucky, Tennessee, and Louisiana are deserving of special mention.

The higher education is not equal to that of England, France, or Germany. Our colleges, numbering more than one hundred and twenty, though possessing more extensive grounds, and often much larger endowments, are not, with a few exceptions, superior, in the extent or thoroughness of their course of instruction, to the collegiate schools of England, the lyceums and colleges of France, or the gymnasia, Real schools, and Latin schools of Germany. Of true university instruction, with the exception of Harvard University, Yale College, and Columbia College, we have nothing deserving the name; and even these are far below the European universities.

But, in the wide diffusion of elementary education, and in the development of a high intellectual activity, no country of Europe can compare favorably with the New England States and New York. A comparison of the percentage of children in attendance upon the schools in these States, to the whole population, with Prussia, Austria, Saxony, and Denmark, where attendance is compulsory, will show conclusively the efficiency of their school organization. Education in the United States, though materially influenced by the writings of Pestalozzi, Fellenberg, and their associates and followers, can hardly be said to be conducted on the Pestalozzian method. The mutual or monitorial system of Lancaster, once very popular here, is now entirely discarded.

The efforts of Woodbridge, Carter, Gallaudet, and others; and, more recently, of Horace Mann, Henry Barnard, David P. Page, Bishop Alonzo Potter, and other eminent friends of education, have accomplished much for the diffusion of right views on the subject of teaching, and have led to the adoption of measures which render our common-school system the glory of our country. In this country, the Sunday-school is not, as in most of the European States, used to impart secular instruction.

Humane and reformatory institutions are quite numerous in the United States: there are more than twenty deaf and dumb institutions, nearly the same number for the blind; seven schools for idiots, and nearly or quite fifty reform schools. Besides the professional seminaries, special schools of military, naval, engineering, chemical, and agricultural science, also exist,—and the last are becoming quite numerous.

The HISPANO-AMERICAN STATES—MEXICO and CENTRAL AMERICA—owing in part to their frequent revolutions, and in part to the large admixture of races, are in a very low educational condition, much lower, even, than when provinces of Spain. No public-school system exists; and, though there are a few good private schools, and some conventual schools, and a university at the city of Mexico, the great mass of the people are most deplorably illiterate.

In the WEST INDIA ISLANDS, CUBA has made some efforts for the improvement of education since 1842, and has now two very good universities and several colleges. The number of elementary schools is estimated at about six hundred, and of pupils not over ten thousand, about one in one hundred of the population. In the rural districts profound ignorance prevails, while in the cities there are a considerable number of good schools. The wealthier classes, very generally, send their children abroad for an education.

In JAMAICA, popular education is more advanced, and a very considerable proportion of the people of color are beginning to understand its advantages. The children in school constitute about one-thirtieth of the whole population. HAYTI has few schools, and no public provision is made for education. The children of the wealthy are generally sent to France for instruction. In the DOMINICAN REPUBLIC, and in PORTO RICO, the schools are few, and generally poor. TRINIDAD has some good schools. The smaller islands have generally made some provision for instruction, though, of course, the advantages are usually limited.

In SOUTH AMERICA, we find the States of NEW GRENADA, VENEZUELA, and ECUADOR possessing few schools, and those of a very inferior character; a very large majority even of the white and creole inhabitants can not read or write, and of the Indians the number who can do so is very small. In FRENCH and DUTCH GUIANA the condition of things is not much better; while in BRITISH GUIANA there are many good schools, and about one in thirteen of the population, including the Indians and negroes, are in attendance upon them. BRAZIL is making great efforts to diffuse education among her people. The emperor is deeply interested in its promotion, and a very efficient system has been organized, but as yet can not be enforced, except in the larger towns. There are colleges, or faculties of science, in most of the principal towns, universities at San Paulo and Pernambuco, and academies or lyceums in the smaller towns. It will be long before schools can be very generally established through the empire, though the large colonies of Germans, which are settling at various points, coming as they do from the best sections of Germany, will render material assistance in the work. At present, not one-sixtieth of the inhabitants are in school.

The Argentine Confederation, and the State of Buenos Ayres, have hitherto paid very little attention to education. The *guachos*, who form a majority of their native population, are a rough, semi-savage race, who care nothing for books, and regard schools with contempt. In BUENOS AYRES, which, with the province of the same name, has recently assumed an independent position, and some of the large towns of the Argentine Confederation, there is a very considerable foreign population, who are generally intelligent, and who have encouraged the establishment of schools of a high grade. The newspaper press of Buenos Ayres is conducted with more ability than that of any other South American city.

URUGUAY possesses even less educational facilities than the Argentine Republic; and the almost constant wars in which it has been engaged for some years past, have tended to reduce its inhabitants to a still lower condition of ignorance. PARAGUAY, on the contrary, has a system of parochial schools, established by the Dictator Francia, and, relatively to most of the other South American States, may be considered as occupying a high rank in the matter of education. CHILE is in advance of any other State of South America, in its educational condition. Its system of schools embraces all grades, from the university to the primary school; and in some of the departments the primary schools are numerous and well conducted; in others, they are not yet generally established; but in all, there is material and decided progress. The classical instruction in her colleges, especially in Latin, would do no discredit to a European college; and her eminent naturalists have diffused a fondness for physical science, which will, ere long, yield abundant results. BOLIVIA and PERU are, like the States north of them, enveloped in ignorance. In the larger towns there are some schools, and in Lima a university, dating from 1551; but so large a proportion of the population of Peru are entirely destitute of education, that in the interior it is difficult to find men who can read and write, to fill the government offices.

The impulse which has been given to education throughout Christendom, within the last fifty years, has already accomplished vast results in improving all the apparatus of instruction and the methods of teaching. In the German States, it has induced thorough professional training, by means of normal schools and teachers' seminaries, the general abandonment of corporal punishment, the introduction of oral exercises, blackboards, and thinking-lessons;—in Great Britain, a reduction of the extreme severities of former times, better qualified teachers, and greatly improved text-books;—in the United States, very great improvements in the architecture of school-houses, in the organization of normal schools, teachers' institutes, and teachers' associations; the introduction of globes, blackboards, charts, &c.; a milder and better discipline, improved methods of teaching, and the substitution of of really scientific and well-adapted text-books for the imperfect and ill-arranged treatises previously in use.

Within a few years past, the competition in the production of school-books has perhaps been carried to an injurious extent; but no one can compare those now in use with those in the schools fifty years since, without becoming satisfied that the progress has been almost miraculous. The danger most to be feared at the present day, in these books, is that the process of simplification may be carried too far, and the pupil be led through a wearisome round of text-books with but little real advancement in knowledge.

The improvement in school-architecture has been very remarkable, especially in the Northern States. The admirable work of Hon. Henry Barnard on this subject has contributed very largely to this result, and has led others recently to enter the same field.

But the most efficient measures for the improvement of education have been the establishment of normal schools, teachers' institutes, and teachers' associations and periodicals. Here new and sound views in regard to instruction, the lessons of experience, and the deductions of science, have been disseminated among thousands of teachers; and thereby the standard of teaching has been greatly elevated, and real progress has been made toward excellence.

In the department of higher education there has also been material advance. The curriculum of study has been enlarged, the requirements for admission raised; the examinations have become true tests of scholarship; higher attainments have been required in the professors; scientific schools have been established in connection with several of the universities, and separate schools of mines, chemistry, physical science, and civil engineering, organized.

Astronomical science, within the past fifty years, has made great progress, both in Europe and America; and in every department of physical research, more has been accomplished than in any previous century.

We may look with certainty for an advance

proportionally much greater, in the coming fifty years. Civilized nations appreciate, as they have never done before, the advantages of education; and, ere long, the teeming millions of China, Japan, and India, driven from their slumber of three thousand years by the impulses of the electric wire and the rush of the locomotive, will join with the enlightened nations of the West, in seeking a higher intellectual development, and the beneficial results of a purer science.

EDUCATIONAL STATISTICS.

WE present a carefully prepared Table showing the educational condition of the different States of the Union about the beginning of 1858. The column of children of school-age embraces all between five and twenty. A part of the States having taken no enumeration of population since 1850, the proportion of scholars to population is not always accurate; and in regard to attendance in the Southern and Western States, we have reason to believe the published reports are frequently defective. We have invariably obtained the latest data to be had, and believe that it will give a more complete estimate of the state of education in the United States than has ever before been presented.

STATISTICS OF EDUCATION IN THE UNITED STATES.

PUBLIC SCHOOLS.

State or Territory.	Area.	Population. Latest Census.	Whole Number of Children of School-Age.	Whole Number of Scholars attending School.
Maine	35,000	583,169	208,854	151,637
New Hampshire.......	8,030	317,976	112,968	96,199
Vermont.............	10,200	314,120	96,568	90,110
Massachusetts.........	7,250	1,133,123	283,000	203,031
Rhode Island..........	1,306	147,545	35,902	26,480
Connecticut	4,750	370,792	111,717	71,269
New York.............	46,000	3,470,459	1,058,324	832,735
Pennsylvania..........	47,000	2,311,786	523,754	598,768
New Jersey...........	6,871	489,555	196,944	129,720
Delaware.............	2,120	91,532	31,544	11,468
Ohio..................	39,964	1,980,329	792,019	603,347
Indiana...............	33,809	988,416	439,257	195,176
Illinois...............	55,409	1,306,576	369,064	323,393
Michigan.............	56,243	511,672	204,268	142,334
Iowa..................	50,914	509,414	195,285	79,672
Wisconsin............	53,924	552,451	241,647	167,110
Missouri	65,037	900,000	302,323	97,907
Kentucky	37,680	982,405	287,212	139,805
Virginia...............	61,352	1,421,661	414,318	49,547
Maryland	11,000	583,034	186,896	33,111
Louisiana	41,346	587,774	96,280	36,000
Tennessee.............	44,000	1,002,717	288,538	126,317
North Carolina	45,000	869,039	245,000	150,000
Georgia...............	58,000	935,090	275,316	77,015
Alabama..............	50,722	841,704	171,073	89,160
South Carolina	30,213	668,507	114,282	19,132
Mississippi............	47,151	606,526	183,903	18,746
Arkansas..............	52,198	247,112	75,000	....
Florida	59,268	110,823	22,512	....
Texas	274,356	212,592	104,313	....
California.............	155,500	507,067	26,170	17,232
			7,694,251	4,576,621

STATISTICS OF EDUCATION IN THE UNITED STATES.

PUBLIC SCHOOLS.

State or Territory.	Amount of Annual Current Expenses for Schools.	Average Wages of Teachers, inclusive of Board.		Amount of School Fund.	Av. No. Months of School per ann.	Av. An. Cost of Tuition to each pupil.
		Males.	Females			
Maine..........	$634,341.89	$27.30	$14.40	$166,346	5.	$2.13
New Hampshire	215,942.00	26.31	14.74	....	5.	2.98
Vermont.......	265,623.00	26.92	15.64	....	5.5	......
Massachusetts..	2,346,309.76	46.63	19.17	1,653,082	7.5	12.
Rhode Island...	167,519.75	34.50	20.34	73,894	8.5	5.60
Connecticut....	358,235.00	30.00	16.00	2,046,397	......	3.02
New York......	3,299,898.93	......	......	2,526,392	7.8	3.97
Pennsylvania...	2,238,840.74	24.00	16.60	....	5.13	7.09
New Jersey.....	503,929.48	32.50	19.75	430,583	9.	5.92
Delaware.......	78,253.14	......	......	440,506	7.6	......
Ohio...........	2,432,069.65	27.71	16.22	....	6.8	3.30
Indiana........	821,713.80	23.76	16.84	4,929,866	3.03	4.21
Illinois.........	302,998.00	25.00	12.00	2,953,594	6.	......
Michigan.......	331,153.89	......	......	1,384,288	5.6	1.6[illegible]
Iowa...........	198,143.00	......	......	2,080,544	......	......
Wisconsin......	484,000.00	27.02	14.92	2,845,846	5.6	2.[illegible]5
Missouri........	436,975.11	......	......	1,500,000	......	......
Kentucky......	304,933.20	......	......	1,455,332	......	3.70
Virginia........	176,645.61	......	......	1,667,652	2.7	2.77
Maryland.......	70,000.00	......	......	150,264	......	......
Louisiana......	312,235.42	......	......	544,692	......	......
Tennessee......	203,197.92	......	......	584,060	......	0.70
North Carolina..	272,320.00	25.00	20.00	2,156,745	4.	1.27
Georgia........	36,236.00	......	......	300,000	......	0.48
Alabama.......	490,690.00	......	......	1,361,137	6.	1.33
South Carolina..	78,338.87	......	......	....	......	4.08
Mississippi.....	81,205.29	......	......	600,000	......	......
Arkansas.......	100,000.00	......	......	2,000,000	......	......
Florida.........	46,060.01	......	......	500,000	......	......
Texas..........	125,000.00	......	......	2,224,806	......	......
California......	156,712.00	......	......	466,000	......	......
	17,559.521 34			36,992,01[illegible]		

We add the following statistics and estimates of instruction in private schools, high-schools, academies, and boarding-schools, and also the latest returns of institutions for higher education, in order to give in one view the magnitude of the educational interest in the United States. The estimates of the number, attendance, and expense of the private schools and schools of higher grade, are deduced from a careful examination of the returns of these schools in four widely separated States, and are believed to be below rather than above the truth.

Number of private schools, high-schools, and academies....	11,500
Average number of pupils, 30 ; total number..............	345,000
Average annual tuition per scholar, $15 ; total expenditure.	$4,575,000
Number of boarding-schools..............................	1,000
Average number of pupils, 50 ; total pupils...............	50,000
Average annual expense of board and tuition, $150 ; total..	$7,500,000

The statistics of higher education are from the latest reports:

	Number of Students.	Annual Expen. per Student.	Total Expenditures.
124 Colleges.....................	13,505	$161	$2,174,305
51 Theological Institutions......	1,520	130	197,600
17 Law Schools.................	1,054	200	210,800
42 Medical Schools.............	4,930	200	986,000
50 Institutions for Blind, Deaf and Dumb, and Idiots..........	4,000	150	600,000
20 Scientific Schools not connected with colleges.......	1,200	200	240,000
			$4,408,705
Add to this the annual expenditure of private and boarding schools, as above..............................			12,075,000
And the aggregate annual expenditure for common-schools, as given in the table above........................			17,559,521
And we have the enormous aggregate of................. as the annual cost of education in the United States.			$34,043,226

BIBLIOGRAPHY.

A FULL bibliography of works on Education would of itself require volumes, and of course our limits preclude any extended list. We only propose to indicate a few of the sources from which we have derived the facts presented in the foregoing treatise, for the use of such of our readers as may be disposed to pursue the subject further.

Of works relating directly to the History of Education, we would specify the following as the most valuable:

FRITZ (Theodore). Système Complet d'Instruction et d'Education. 3 vols.........................*Strasbourg*, 1843.

SCHWARZ (J. G. C.). Erziehungslehre. 2 vols..*Leipsic*, 1829.

DE RIANCY. Histoire de la Liberté d'Enseignement....*Paris*.

OZANAM. La Civilization au V[ième.] Siècle. 2 vols.....*Paris*.

DE VIRIVILLE. Instruction Publique en Europe..*Paris*, 1852.

PERRY (W. C.). German University Education.*London*, 1845.

MALDEN. Origin of Universities..............*London*, 1849.

SCHMIDT. History of Education. (Harper's Family Library).....................................*New York*.

HALLAM (Sir Henry). History of Literature in the 15th and 16th Centuries. American edition.............*New York*.

SISMONDI (J. C.). Literature of the South of Europe. American edition. . . . . *New York.*
TICKNOR (George). History of Spanish Literature. . . . *Boston.*

Of Historical works bearing upon the subject incidentally, the number is very great. The following as well as many others were consulted:

NIEBUHR'S Ancient History. 3 vols. Am. ed. . *Philadelphia.*
DEW'S Ancient and Modern Nations. . . . . *New York.*
XENOPHON'S Anabasis.
GROTE'S Greece. Am. ed. 12 vols. . . . . *New York.*
THIRLWALL'S Greece. Am. ed. 2 vols. . . . . "
NIEBUHR'S Rome. Am. ed. 3 vols. . . . . *Philadelphia.*
ARNOLD'S Rome. Am. ed. 3 vols. . . . . *New York.*
LIDDELL'S Rome. Am. ed. 1 vol. . . . . "
GIBBON'S Decline and Fall. Milman's notes. 6 vols. "
HUME'S England. Am. ed. 6 vols. . . . . "
MACAULAY'S England. Am. ed. 4 vols. . . . . "
LINGARD'S England. Am. ed. 13 vols. . . . . *Boston.*
MICHELET'S France. Am. ed. 3 vols. . . . . *New York.*
KOHLRAUSCH'S Germany. 1 vol. Am. ed. . . . . "
NEANDER'S Church History. 5 vols. Am. ed. . . . . *Boston.*
MOSHEIM'S Church History. 3 vols. Am. ed. . . . . *New York.*
SCHAFF'S Church History. 1 vol. Am. ed. . . . . "
HASE'S Church History. 1 vol. Am. ed. . . . . "
GIESELER'S Church History. 6 vols. . . . . *Edinburgh.*
WILSON'S India. 1 vol. . . . . *New York.*
MURRAY'S India. 1 vol. . . . . *London.*
WILLIAMS' Middle Kingdom. 1 vol. . . . . *New York.*
CULBERTSON'S Flowery Land. 1 vol. . . . . "
HILDRETH'S Japan. 1 vol. . . . . *Boston.*
PERRY'S Japan. 1 vol. . . . . *New York.*
SMYTH'S Lectures on Modern History. 2 vols. . . . . *London.*

WILKINSON'S Ancient Egyptians. 2 vols. Am. ed..*New York.*
KENRICK'S Egypt under the Pharaohs. 2 vols. " "
TENNEMAN'S History of Philosophy. 1 vol..........*London.*
LEWES' Biographical History of Philosophy. 1 vol..*New York.*
WHEWELL'S History of the Inductive Sciences. 2 vols. "
PLINY THE ELDER'S Natural History. Translated by Bostoch and Riley......................................*London.*
PLINY THE YOUNGER'S Epistles. Trans. by Melmoth.. "
HALLAM'S History of the Middle Ages. 1 vol......*New York.*
PRESCOTT'S Conquest of Mexico. 3 vols.............*Boston.*
" Conquest of Peru. 2 vols................ "
CONDE'S Arabs in Spain. 3 vols...................*London.*

In General Literature, Travels, etc., the following with many others have been consulted:

IRVING'S (W.) Mohammed and his Successors. 2 vols..*New York.*
" " Conquest of Granada. 1 vol........ "
LAYARD'S Nineveh. 1 vol. Am. ed.............. "
" Nineveh and Babylon. 1 vol.............*London.*
LOFTUS' Susiana. 1 vol. Am. ed................*New York.*
LIVINGSTON'S Africa. 1 vol. Am. ed............. "
ERMAN'S Siberia 2 vols. Am. ed.............*Philadelphia.*
ATKINSON'S Siberia. 1 vol. Am. ed.............*New York.*
BARTH'S Central Africa. 3 vols. Am. ed......... "
WILSON'S Africa. 1 vol........................ "
BOWEN'S Central Africa. 1 vol.................*Charleston.*
KIDDER & FLETCHER'S Brazil. 1 vol...........*Philadelphia.*
PAGE'S La Plata. 1 vol........................*New York.*
BRACE'S Norse Folk. 1 vol..................... "
BAYARD TAYLOR'S Travels. 6 vols............... "
GILLISS' (Lieutenant). Astronomical Expedition to Chili. 3 vols...................................*Washington.*

Of Biographical works, the following Biographical Dictionaries have been freely consulted, as well as numerous particular biographies:

BIOGRAPHIE GÉNÉRALE. 45 vols...................... *Paris.*
BIOGRAPHIE UNIVERSELLE. 118 vols................. "
GORTON'S Biographical Dictionary. 4 vols.......... *London.*
ROSE'S Biographical Dictionary. 12 vols........... "
THE ENGLISH CYCLOPEDIA—Biographical Section. 6 vols. "
BLAKE'S Biographical Dictionary. New ed. 1 vol.... *Phila.*
APPLETON'S Cyclopedia of Biography. 1 vol...... *New York.*

The following Periodicals have also been of great service:

BARNARD'S American Journal of Education. First series. 5 vols..................................... *Hartford.*
AMERICAN EDUCATIONAL ALMANAC—1858 .... *Boston.*
AMERICAN ALMANAC—1859........................ "
MANN'S (Hon. Horace) Reports on Education—1838–48. "
EDUCATIONAL REPORTS of Canadian School System and of the Superintendents for 1856–7–8................... *Toronto.*
STATE EDUCATIONAL PERIODICALS for 1858.
ANNUAIRE D'EDUCATION EN FRANCE—1858............ *Paris.*

Reference has also been made to BARNARD'S "Education in Europe," "Normal Schools," and "Papers on Reformatory Education," etc., and to several of the works of Pestalozzi, Niemeyer, Blochmann, Diesterweg, and others named in the body of this work.

INDEX.

www.ingramcontent.com/pod-product-compliance
Lightning Source LLC
LaVergne TN
LVHW020238110826
845151LV00003B/958

* 9 7 8 1 4 2 5 5 2 9 3 4 5 *